Elena Tzareva

RUGS & CARPETS FROM CENTRAL ASIA

THE RUSSIAN COLLECTIONS

ALLEN LANE / PENGUIN BOOKS
AURORA ART PUBLISHERS, LENINGRAD

Designed by Gennady Yabkevich and
Irina Luzhina

Translated from the Russian by
Arthur Shkarovsky-Raffé

The author is grateful to Mr. Robert Pinner for his
detailed reading of the text. The Publishers would also
like to thank Mr. David Black and Mr. Clive Loveless for
their invaluable advice.

Penguin Books Ltd, Harmondsworth,
Middlesex, England

Penguin Books, 40 West 23rd Street, New York,
New York 10010, U.S.A.

Penguin Books Australia Ltd, Ringwood,
Victoria, Australia

Penguin Books Canada Ltd, 2801 John Street, Markham,
Ontario, Canada L3R 1B4

Penguin Books (N.Z.) Ltd, 182-190 Wairau Road,
Auckland 10, New Zealand

Published by Allen Lane/Penguin Books 1984

Created by Aurora Art Publishers, Leningrad, for joint
production of Aurora and Penguin Books Limited/Allen
Lane

Penguin ISBN 014 00 6369 2
Allen Lane ISBN 0 7139 1504 8

Printed and bound in Austria by Globus, Vienna

A genuinely academic study of Oriental carpets and rugs began in the last half of the nineteenth century, which likewise witnessed the publication of the first works ever to deal with Central Asian weavings written by Russian art historians and collectors. Thus, published at the turn of this century were works on the subject by A. A. Bogolyubov, A. A. Felkerzam, S. M. Dudin and A. A. Semionov[1], that are still valid as they outlined ways and means of research in classifying this highly intricate and anonymous art. Of particular importance were the writings of a gifted Soviet scholar V. G. Moshkova, whose *Tribal Göls in Turkoman Carpets* and *Carpets and Rugs of the Peoples of Central Asia*[2] are to this day fundamental studies second to none in the information they provide.

West European interest in Central Asian carpets arose in the 1960s and 1970s and is still growing with more and more collectors attracted by their peculiar beauty and superb technique employed by their weavers. Besides, these wonderful works of folk art can reveal much about the life and traditions of the people who made them. Thus, now, a carpet specialist can determine when a carpet or rug was knotted, by whom, how many women wove it, whether it was made for domestic use or for the market, etc. Yet, much is still obscure as there is but little evidence to proceed from to date an item, identify the appearance of an old Central Asian carpet and its ornamental design, or ascertain the impact of inter-tribal influences. No wonder carpet specialists are so greatly attracted to the Central Asian carpet and endeavour to seek out unpublished items to draw comparisons. Now we may say that the Central Asian carpet and rug are gradually, though tardily, disclosing their secrets and providing valuable information about their makers.

Nomadic Central Asia was in all likelihood one of the centres where the craft of pile weaving either originated or was perfected. Not only the climate but also the specific nomadic way of life played a definite role. The need to warm the *yurt* in the colder seasons suggested production of felted and knotted rugs and carpets. Considering the abundance of wool in a pastoral economy they were more reasonable to make. However, whereas felted mattings and flatweaves were produced throughout Central Asia, pile weaving was mostly practised by the Turkomans on the south-eastern coast of the Caspian Sea, at the foothills of the Kopet-dag range and in the valleys of the Atrek, Sumbar, Tejen, Murgab, and Amu-Darya rivers; by the Uzbeks living around Bukhara and Samarkand and by groups of the Kazakhs, Kirghiz, Karakalpaks and Baluch inhabiting the Kyzyl-Kum desert, the highlands near Samarkand, the Ferghana and Hissar valleys, and also along the lower reaches of the Syr-Darya.

As carpet making emerged amidst different peoples in these areas at different times, regional levels are naturally dissimilar. Evidently first to practise the craft were the Turkomans who inherited the technique either from Persian ancestors inhabiting this region from the 2nd millennium B.C., or from the Turko-Oghuz, who, overrunning Central Asia in the 9th century A.D., comprised the nucleus of

6

the Turkoman nation. It is likely that both were important to the development of pile weaving. At any rate, two traditional lines are to be observed in pile-woven articles made prior to the beginning of this century, corresponding to the two ancient—Salor and Chodor[3]—tribal federations; this is especially evident in the colour schemes, a red ground of the central field being characteristic of the Salor and the purple-brown of the Chodor. Quite likely the two types of knots— symmetrical (*duochitme*) and asymmetrical (*yarachitme*)—are also indicative of diverse traditions.

The insular mode of life of Central Asia's nomads was responsible for the appearance of certain characteristic features in the artistic aspect and technique of carpet making. This is more strikingly manifest amidst peoples that preserved a certain tribal isolation right up to the twentieth century. Thus, we may currently identify Kirghiz, Kazakh, Karakalpak, Uzbek, Baluch and Turkoman rugs and carpets. Carpet scholars have accepted a division by tribe in Turkoman carpets and rugs which identifies a number of groups, including, e.g., those of the Salor, Saryk, Tekke, Yomud and Ersari. Yet, whereas Salor and Saryk pieces can be related specifically to the tribes named, the produce of the other three groups cannot be easily identified. The Ersari, for example, comprise a complex ethnic fusion of residual indigenous population and intruding Turkomans. Tribal groups of the Ersari, Sakar, Salor, Kizil Ayak, Olam and Karkin—to mention but a few—who inhabited the middle reaches of the Amu-Darya shared common economic and political interests. Hence, it is quite possible that from the eighteenth century the making of carpets and rugs, especially for the market, also went along common lines. Thus amidst the Ersari, there existed such sub-groups as, for instance, the Kizil Ayak and Arabatchi. Economic hardships and political upheavals induced numerous smaller tribes to accede to such large tribal federations as the Tekke and Yomud. Indeed, in the carpets and rugs made by these groups, which are highly diversified in both ornamental pattern and technique, one distinctly discerns foreign features.

Until recently, attribution of Central Asian carpets and rugs to one or another tribe was most inaccurate. In the literature, especially that of a popular kind, such terms as Pende, Bashir, Bukhara and the like are still common. In some cases (Pende and Bashir, for instance) the names of the carpets and rugs derive from their places of origin. In other cases (Bukhara, for example) the name is actually that of the place where the pieces were sold. Indeed, Bukhara has been from time immemorial a major centre where rugs and carpets were marketed, though pile weaving was not practised even in its vicinity, let alone in the town itself. There were, of course, cases when buyers deliberately changed the names in order to conceal the source of merchandise—which is apparently why quite a few Uzbek carpets were attributed to the Karakalpaks, and why there is still confusion on this point.

Another accepted tradition is to classify the rugs and carpets of Central Asia according to type. Thus Turkomans called the large main carpets which were produced everywhere the *khali* while all others termed them the *gilim* or *giliam*. The Turkomans, Kirghiz and Uzbek Turkman living in and around Nurata made such main carpets basically in one piece, whereas the Kazakhs, Karakalpaks and Uzbeks living elsewhere stitched them together of strips woven in a mixed technique. Also common with the Uzbeks were stitched high-pile main carpets which they called the *julkhyrs*. The Kirghiz started to make main carpets much later in the nineteenth century, possibly even in its second half, as is borne out by the specific ornamental designs and technique. Among the most interesting are the main carpets of the Kirghiz Khydyrsha tribe. Often modelled on a definite prototype, they were extremely large, at times several dozen square metres in area; their weavers called them the *sarai kilem* ('palace carpets').

The nomads also made many other items from pile-woven textiles for domestic use. Especially was this true of the Turkomans. Thus one may mention the *ensi*, decorative tent-door hanging, in which many elements of the ornamental design were protective symbols introduced to ward off evil spirits. The Kirghiz also wove similar door curtains which they called the *eshik tysh*. The Turkomans had the *kapunuk*, tent-door surround, and the *germetch*, threshold rug. All three, the *ensi*,

Summer encampment of the Kirghiz. 1902

8

Turkoman woman weaving a chuval tent bag. The Merv oasis. 1902

kapunuk and *germetch*, as well as the *dezlik* of the Tekke tribe, integrated into one composite ensemble, wherein the arrangement of the designs and their various components accentuated and complemented one another.

Common among all the peoples of Central Asia were various bags, of different size and shape, which were hung on the inside of the tent wall and served as containers for clothes and household utensils. The Turkomans called them the *chuval*, *torba* and *mafrach*, the Uzbeks—the *napramach* and *karchin*, the Karakalpaks—the *karshin*, the Kirghiz—the *chavadan* and the Kazakhs—the *shabadan*. Likewise common were smaller bags—especially diversified among the Turkomans—including the long *aina khalta* bag for mirrors, the round stitched *igsalik*, bag for spindles, and the *bukhcha*, cases for books.

All the nomadic peoples in this area produced decorative strips and bands which were used to strengthen the wooden frames of the *yurt* (the Turkomans termed them the *iolam* and other peoples, the *baskur*). With the Kazakhs and Karakalpaks these comprised the bulk of the pile weavings made. The Turkomans also wove hanging *sallanchak*, cradles, *ayatlyk*, funerary rugs, and U-shaped *ojakbashi*, hearth surrounds. Made in some places, primarily along the banks of the

Amu-Darya, were *namazlyk*, prayer rugs and pairs of hangings of a special design that were used to decorate the smoke hole of the *yurt*.

The nomads also adorned their camels, horses and donkeys. The woven decorations included trappings, *eyerlik*, saddle coverings and *khurjin*, paired saddlebags, which were made throughout Central Asia. Special care was taken with camel trappings for a wedding caravan. The leading camel carrying the bridal litter was covered with twin flank trappings of a rectangular, pentagonal or heptagonal shape called the *asmalyk*. The animal's knees were adorned with heavily tasselled pile ribbons and a kind of cap was placed on its head. Suspended from the sides of the nuptial *kejebe*, litter, were round long *uuk bash*, bags to hold the tent poles. Suspended from the camel's neck was a *dezlik* (*khalyk*) hanging, which the bride had to weave herself; as soon as she arrived this piece would be hung over the *ensi* on the door of the groom's tent with the back displayed, thereby to enable every guest to appreciate the bride's skill.

While carpets, rugs and other pile articles comprised part of the dowry even among sedentary tribes, with nomads the number of woven items in the dowry was strictly regulated, including, as a rule, the most beautiful pieces.

In Central Asia, carpet making has always been an exclusively female craft. The technique was handed down from mother to daughter, along with such aesthetic notions as the favourite composition, design and colour range. The craft has always been highly esteemed, with romantic legends told about especially gifted weavers. The loveliest pieces were jealously preserved family heirlooms that were passed down from generation to generation. In this manner the Turkomans preserved their supreme achievement, the carpets and rugs woven by the Salor.

Little girls were instructed in the rudiments of the craft from the age of seven or nine. They were first taught to weave, after which they gradually learned the other related techniques, with dyeing as the most complex, learned last. Carpet weaving was an onerous, tiring craft, so much so that the weaver could consider herself master only after she reached the age of twenty-five. As the years rolled by powers ebbed and eyesight weakened; yet even the elderly contributed, with blind old women spinning thread.

The range of tools was extremely small—a loom, a knife, a pair of scissors, a comb to beat down the weft, a cord to protect the weft from damage and warp wideners. The loom is, generally, a simple device, indeed so crude with nomadic tribes, that it is hard to imagine how it could have served to manufacture such marvellous pieces. It consisted of two poles that were imbedded in the ground parallel to one another; the warp threads were stretched across on them as on a frame. Turkoman poles were square. The beams were greased with clay to hold the warp threads in a definite order. However, the Ferghana Kirghiz and Samarkand Uzbeks made looms from easily available bits and pieces, which, naturally, often affected quality. Despite their crudeness they all met one requirement—they were convenient to transport. Whenever the tribe moved, the warp together with the woven portion was wound round the top of the loom into a compact bundle.

We have been discussing thus far narrow-beam looms used to weave small pieces of not more than 1.5 metres across. Stationary broad-beam looms that are employed to make main carpets were set up in the nomadic encampments either in a special *yurt*, under a temporary canopy, or in the shade of trees. If it was desired to weave a carpet of a larger size, with which one or two carpet makers would be unable to cope within the available time, relatives and neighbours would be asked to help.

In regions, where pile weaving was well-developed, so much time was devoted to the craft that as soon as a girl started weaving independently she would be able to reproduce from memory virtually any of the designs she had seen. Now and again she might draw upon a model that had taken her fancy, as she often had collections of bits and pieces of old carpets and rugs. Yet whether she copied from a model or reproduced a design from memory, carpet weaving was a creative process, and we will never find two absolutely identical old carpets (except for those deliberately made in pairs).

The fact that carpet-weavers were so easily able to reproduce any design has made it difficult for carpet scholars to determine the age of pieces. Thus, a design characteristic of one tribe may often appear on carpets and rugs made by another. In smaller pieces, made towards the close of the nineteenth century, one finds both

Kirghiz women weaving a carpet. 1900s

archaic and contemporary elements coexisting in the ornamental design of the central field. Specific tribal features are more often observed in the borders and *elem* end panels.

In the carpet-making areas, among the nomadic peoples that had preserved a tribal division right up to the beginning of this century, definite ornamental elements are employed exclusively for decorating main carpets. The Turkomans have a special term for these elements, the *göl*.

Unlike tapestry weaving, knotting allows of only a few variations. In Central Asia there are two types of pile weaving. A pile textile is actually a length of plain-woven fabric but with rows of knots tied around pairs of warp threads between the weft threads. The piece is woven from the outset in virtually the same manner as a tapestry, with sufficiently thick, tightly twisted warp threads stretched across the loom to make a tapestry-type plain weave end which, depending upon the item, may be from two to four centimetres long or, in case of the main carpet, as much as fifty to sixty centimetres. With some peoples the material and colour of the warp were strictly defined. Thus the Turkomans always employed wool which would usually be white in pieces made by the Salor, Saryk and Tekke, and could be of different tints in the carpets of other tribes. Starting in the second half of the nineteenth century, the Kirghiz, Uzbeks and Kazakhs began to use cotton warps.

When the tapestry-type portion is of the desired length, pile knotting commences. In the case of double-level knotting the pile yarn loops the upper and lower warp rows covering them from the back. In the case of single-level knotting the pile yarns are tied only to the upper warp threads and from the back the knot is seen as a dot. The ends of the pile threads are cut with a knife, after which the entire row is trimmed with a pair of scissors. When a row of knots is completed, the weft is passed once or twice and the pile is beaten down with a heavy comb. However, to avoid damaging the warp threads, a thick soft cord is stretched above the weft prior to beating.

With different tribes the number of weft shoots, the general quality and the colour of the material varied. Thus, some two-thirds of Kirghiz carpets have only one weft shoot. However, in old Salor and Saryk carpets and rugs, there are always two weft shoots of brown wool. The Chodor often employed camel hair twisted with white cotton thread as the weft. The greater the knot density, the thinner the weft and warp yarns and the more weakly are they twisted; the smaller the density, the coarser are the foundation yarns.

In the case of single level knotting (knots over three warps) the asymmetrical knot open on the right was usually employed; less frequently the symmetrical knot was used with a single weft shoot. In these cases the weft would loop the upper and lower warp rows thus enabling pile knotting to be combined with tapestry weaving. This technique was extensively utilized by the tribes of Central Asia to make tent bands, while sometimes strips made in this technique were stitched to produce carpets and hangings. Uzbek *julkhyrses* were executed by means of the same technique but unlike other stitched pieces the entire surface was knotted in pile according to a pre-conceived design. The *julkhyrs* has a characteristic shaggy, untrimmed pile, up to fifteen millimetres long, that was responsible for the name, as *julkhyrs* translates as 'bearskin'. The primitiveness of this technique warrants the assumption postulated by many carpet experts that it must be of an archaic order.

In double-level knotting two knot types were employed by Central Asian nomadic weavers, notably asymmetrical and symmetrical knots. The assymmetrical knot could be open on the left or the right.

The symmetrical knot was used by the Saryk and a large proportion of the Yomud, and was also employed on some asymmetrical knotted Tekke and Yomud pieces for vertical selvedge rows. All other tribes employed the asymmetrical knot, primarily open on the right. The traditional use of different types of knots by various tribes greatly facilitates attribution of pile-woven articles.

Knot density and pile height depended on the function of the article and the skill of the weaver. In main carpets the density, as a rule, rarely exceeded 2,500 knots per square decimetre, with the pile three to four millimetres high. In Turkoman rugs and carpets the density was usually between 1,000 and 3,000 knots per square decimetre with the pile upto five to six millimetres high. With other

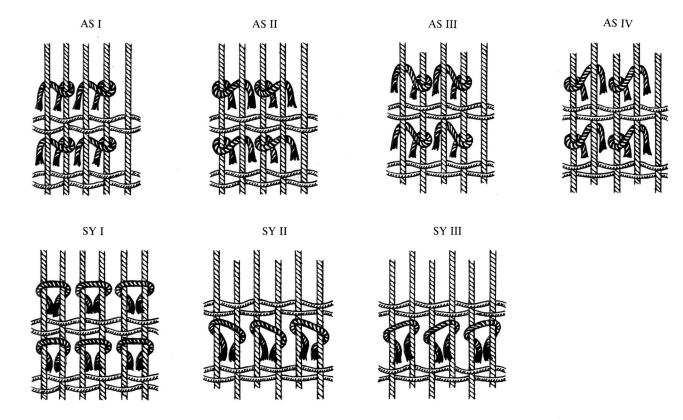

AS I   AS II   AS III   AS IV

SY I   SY II   SY III

peoples it was rarely above 1,000 knots and the pile was often considerably higher. However, in small pieces where a high pile was not required, the knot density was often far greater. As less time was needed to weave smaller items, their makers demonstrated greater care, choosing a more complex design that necessitated a greater knot density. Thus in the small carpet products of the Kirghiz, Uzbeks, and Karakalpaks the number of knots per square decimetre may reach as high as 2,500. On the other hand, small Turkoman pieces normally have knot densities between 1,500 and 4,000 or more knots per square decimetre depending on the weaving to be. We also know of a group of *torbas* with an average knot density over 5,000 and of some specimens with a knot density of 10,000 per square decimetre.

Apart from wool, extensive use was made of silk and cotton for the pile. The silk was mostly dyed pink or scarlet and less often sky-blue and yellow, while the cotton was bleached. The combination of sparkling silk and matted cotton made the woven items look festive.

Red is the universally dominant colour both in small pieces and main carpets, except for some Yomud, mostly Ogurdjali, *asmalyks*, Ersari, mostly Bashir, *namazlyks* and some Kirghiz main carpets. The prevalence of white, mid-blue and sky-blue in the last two cases mentioned is a latter-day untraditional innovation.

The impression of an overall red colouring was achieved by filling the central field and some individual elements of the ornamental design with yarns of this colour. Various factors were responsible for the choice of colours.

Knot types:
Asymmetrical knots
Symmetrical knots

pl. 54

14

In Central Asia, as in many other places for that matter, red symbolizes life, prosperity, and the sun; its dominance corresponds to traditional aesthetic notions. However, there were undoubtedly practical reasons as well. Weavers did not have available any too broad an assortment of colours; the natural tints of wool are white and brown, while natural dyes give yellows, oranges, various shades of red, mid- and sky-blue and greens. White and yellow easily soil, while brown is too sombre. Blues and green could be obtained only by employing the costly imported indigo. Moreover, weavers did not know how to use the indigo and either bought ready-dyed wool, or farmed the wool out to urban dyers. There remained red which was extracted from the local madder root, which depending on its age yielded a wide range of shades from a light red to a violet-brown.

Throughout the region darker colours were employed to outline the ornamental components, and the brighter colours, such as yellow, orange, sky-blue and white, to fill in the details of the design. A common practice with all, strictly adhered to by the Turkomans, was the use of two or three shades of red. In the case of a dark ground the ornamental components were picked out in brighter colours; in the case of a light ground the design was executed in a dark red or violet-brown.

Interior of a Turkoman yurt. 1900

This colour range was natural for the linear ornamental designs common to Central Asian carpets and rugs. By colouring identical design elements differently, weavers achieved an impression of richness despite the limited assortment of only five–ten colours. The introduction of the ground colour into the contoured designs of the central field and borders imparts an unusual, enigmatic appeal, producing an impression of a floating, moving ornament, enhanced when Turkoman weavers employed their favourite technique of a diagonal colour scheme.

Two different compositions dominate the carpet products of Central Asia. One is to arrange the design in rows—especially common in tent bands and articles made up from them. The number of ornamental designs is of the order of several score. Thus in Karakalpak tent bands there exist up to sixty different patterns, each with its own specific name. With most peoples the prevalent motif was a pair of horns in different versions. The design was organized around a diamond or transversely. As a rule bands were woven in a mixed technique with white woollen or cotton yarn used for warp and weft. The combination of unpatterned white ground with a polychrome pile design imparted a sense of richness, making the bands the paramount adornment of the *yurt* interior. Analogous compositions of a

pls. 64, 65, 85–88, 126

At the bazaar in Ashkhabad. 1960s

striped design will be observed likewise in fully pile-woven items, whose ornamentation is akin to that of embroideries and tapestries; most likely it was influenced by the latter, even though in a greatly modified manner.

pls. 53, 141

The other main design composition—which is to be observed in all other pieces—is to divide the ornamented surface into a central field and framing borders. The central field may differ in shape; it may be rectangular, pentagonal, or seven sided in camel and horse trappings and Π-shaped in door hangings. Old carpets never had more than three borders but late-nineteenth century pieces may have as many as twelve. This increase in the number of borders was caused by the demand of the market for a much greater knot density which in turn tended to reduce the size of the articles with the design proportions remaining unchanged. So, to retain the previous size, the number of borders was increased, which not infrequently distorted the traditional composition.

The introduction of an additional end border is characteristic of all types of articles—except for the *julkhyrs*, some Uzbek main carpets and Kirghiz carpet products.

The design arrangement depended primarily on the function of the article. In main carpets it adhered to the principle of symmetry since the carpet occupied the centre of the *yurt* and had to look the same from both ends. However, in hangings the lower portion of the composition was emphasized by introducing an additional end panel which the Turkomans called the *elem*.

The principles of a well-proportioned compositional arrangement, choice of ornamental pattern and colouring comprised one integral system. In many items, especially in Turkoman pieces, some designs in the central field corresponded to distinct motifs in both the main and additional borders.

There are five known types of composition for the central field in Central Asian carpets and rugs, namely, the medallion, the lattice, the U-shape, the arch and the panel. Commonest is the medallion which weavers of all ethnic units employ to adorn both main carpets and small pieces. The pattern in this case consists of horizontal or diagonal rows of medallions alternating with rows of secondary motifs. The Turkomans and Uzbek Turkman used *göls* to ornament their main carpets; these are octagonal or diamond-shaped figures with complex symmetrical fillings with a diagonally coloured centre and stylized representations of birds and animals. Each Turkoman tribe had one or several *göls* which served as their emblems. They were usually called after the name of the tribe—such as the

pls. 28, 31, 32; 114, 115

pl. 118

Tekke *göl* or the Chodor *göl*. The name the Uzbek Turkman gave their *göl*, the *kalkan nuska*, actually means 'shield', and it is quite likely that it indeed represented a shield with the tribal emblem.

pls. 70; 67, 68

pls. 66, 69

In cases when a tribe had several such emblems each had a definite name. Thus the Yomud had the *kapsa göl* and *dyrnak göl*. They also employed in their main carpets other *göl*-like designs which were mostly decorative. Evidently they were introduced to meet market requirements. Although the Yomud preserved their natural economy till the close of the nineteenth century, they began to manufacture

carpets for sale, chiefly for Caucasian and Persian markets, earlier and more energetically than other Turkoman tribes. Apparently their use of several *göls* is also due to their having incorporated several smaller tribes.

Strolling acrobats and musicians giving a performance. Tashkent. 1901

In cases when a tribal federation was of long standing, the original names of the design and of the tribe that had created it would be forgotten; now the design would be named after some characteristic feature. The *göl* was only used on main carpets while the tribe was still politically independent. If the tribe lost its independence its *göl* was either consigned to oblivion or re-interpreted as a motif for the decoration of other items, primarily the *chuval* tent bags. It was now seen as a version of the *chuval göl*, or named after the place where it was commonest or after the tribe using it oftenest. Apparently something of this nature must have happened to the Salor *göl*. For long it was revered as a tribal emblem, although not one old Salor *khali* carpet possessing this design is known; on the contrary, it was already known as the Mary *göl*. It has now been established that the Salor tribal emblem is of a totally different contour and is more reminiscent of the Ersari *gülli göl*, whereas the so-called Salor *göl* is either the emblem of a tribe once incorporated in the Salor federation, or, which is more likely, a version of a motif

pls. 24, 25
pls. 2, 3

that the Salor employed to decorate their tent bags. This would also be the reason why it was used by other tribes.

On the whole, the ornamentation of Salor main carpets is conspicuous for a degree of stability, amazing even for the Turkomans: they have the same version of the *göl*, a distinctive secondary motif and identical borders. The archaic impression that the Salor ornamental pattern produces is not fortuitous; it is confirmed by analogous representations on other early Turkoman carpets.[4] Generally Salor designs are of great interest not only by virtue of their beauty and diversity but also as a source of information on early Turkoman carpet design in general. In the early 1830s the Salor were beset by a series of tragic misfortunes that almost wiped them out. As the Turkomans regard the Salor as the originators of pile weaving, their pieces were preserved by neighbouring tribes and many have survived.

pl. 10
pl. 15
pl. 10

Besides the various *göls*, medallion compositions also drew upon rosettes of elaborate contours that were always accompanied by arches with a zoomorphic filling which lent the name of *kejebe* to the composition. The *kejebe* has two variations of the central medallion, one for smaller *torbas*, the other for large bags or *asmalyks*. Their salient feature is a broad U-shaped *khamtoz elem* panel filling the lower part of the *torba*. Some scholars believe the Salor used these *torbas* as *asmalyks* and we have reasons to accept that assumption, as the singular composition of the central field and the unusually large size of such *torbas* indicate a very special designation.

pls. 117, 119, 120, 134, 136, 148

As a rule, the Uzbeks, Kirghiz, Karakalpaks and Kazakhs employed geometrical designs in the medallion compositions of their main carpets and bags—except for the pattern of stylized zoomorphic figures common to the Karakalpaks decorating the central field of the *karshin* bags. Of definite symbolical meaning were the rosettes with the *muiiz* horns that were characteristic of all the ethnic groups listed.

pls. 127, 131

pls. 130, 148

pls. 6–9, 20–23, 26, 27, 48–52, 54, 79, 80, 111

Most frequently employed on *chuvals* and *torbas* with a medallion composition were variations of the *chuval göl*, namely medallions of a tribal *göl*-type. Meanwhile the secondary motifs were either chuval *göls* of simpler outline or crosslike *chemche* designs. The Turkomans frequently drew upon the Salor *göl*, of which the most interesting variant, almost square in form, is to be observed on Salor *chuvals*. Here the secondary element is the *charkh palak* figure. Quite probably the name harks back to the original meaning of this cruciform composition, which many peoples regarded as a representation of the Universe. The motif was also common with the Saryk. The latter apparently borrowed it together with other ornaments for the central field. These designs almost completely replaced the older motifs, after the Saryk came into close contact with the Salor in the nineteenth century. Indeed, today it is extremely difficult to find traditional compositions and patterns in Saryk pile-carpet articles. We are of the belief that the design on the *torba* in plate 27 is authentically Saryk.

pl. 27

The straight and diagonal lattice designs are evidently the earliest of those listed. In Turkoman pieces, having a diagonal lattice design, we find the *ak su*, *shemle* and *dogajik* motifs, which were employed to decorate the central field of *torbas*, *kapunuks*, *dezliks* and *asmalyks*. With some other Central Asian tribes a lattice design is to be observed on large main carpets. pls. 119, 137, 147

All Central Asian tribes employed the *dogajik* motif, in various combinations pl. 77 and variously interpreted, to decorate both the central field and borders. Extremely interesting is one special compositional arrangement which only the Tekke use to ornament the central field in *asmalyks*. This is a diagonal lattice design composed of figures reminiscent of elongated, toothed leaves. Inscribed within the compartments are either birds or large flowers symmetrically flanked by small representa- pls. 43, 44, 46 tions of animals. The composition in such pieces is always the same, with the pl. 45 *ovadan* motif on a white ground in the main border and the *elem* panel narrow and unembellished. The bird motif is evidently among the oldest extant.

Designs based on straight lattices are less common. As a rule, compartments were filled with repeated geometrical motifs usually in diagonal rows of alternating colours. Straight lattice designs were also employed to decorate the central field of

In the workshop of the Turkmenkovior firm. 1970s

pls. 5, 30, 55, 56, 62

pls. 135, 138

large main carpets and to embellish small pieces. Commonest with the Salor and Tekke was the *aina khamtoz* motif; meanwhile the *aina kochak* motif is used exclusively by the Tekke. Widespread in Kirghiz main carpets was a compositional arrangement with a straight lattice design filled with floral motifs.

A П-shaped arrangement of the central field design is characteristic of three types of door hangings namely the *ensi, kapunuk* and *dezlik*. Here the patterns are traditional, with a minimum number of variations for each tribe. *Ensi* designs are extremely complex and contain a great variety of motifs that are not to be observed on other pieces. Typical of the older *ensi* is the base panel ("ground") with flowers in its lower portion, and an arch with the *sainak* motifs enclosing the entire composition in the upper portion and the *ovadan* meander (symbolizing the eternity of life). Some components suggest that the compositional arrangement of the *ensi* reflects the Turkomans' concept of the Universe: the space within the arch is filled with symbolical representations of creatures of vital significance for the Turkomans, notably rams (the *sainak* horn and zoomorphic figures), birds (bands with symmetrically arranged bird heads), and dogs (the central panel with the *gujuk izy* motif). There is reason to believe that the *kelle* motif in some variations designates people, not flowers. The aforementioned elements have been preserved best in the designs of Salor and Saryk hangings. However, the second third of the nineteenth century saw a gradual departure from the classical compositional arrangement of the *ensi* that was followed by its complete abandonment.

pls. 17, 18
pls. 16, 34, 71
pls. 35, 72, 73, 102
pls. 4, 19

In this book *kapunuk* design is exemplified exclusively by the *ovadan* motif which is characteristic of all Turkoman tribes, though we may also find the *ak su* ("white water") motif which is of magical importance insofar as white—in other words, fresh—water has always been a source of life for Central Asian peoples.

pl. 11

The *dezlik*, which was hung above the tent-door and of which mainly Tekke examples are known, was decorated with three types of motifs that possessed the protective significance of a guardian spirit and that, as a rule, were integrated into one definite compositional arrangement. Only one example of these designs is represented here.

pls. 39–41

Characteristic of the Kirghiz *eshik tysh* hanging is an arched arrangement of the basic motif and a white ground for the central field.

pl. 140

The Ersari mainly drew upon the arched compositional arrangement to decorate their *namazlyks*. Here the basic element of the central field is an arch which is created either by several narrow borders or by one or two broader bands.

pls. 98–100

All the related elements are, as a rule, of a floral character and the designs of the borders usually differ from those of the central field. One exception, however, is the unique *namazlyk*, the entire surface of which, except for the elegant slender arch based on the *giyak* motif, is filled with repeated stylized plant ornaments.

pl. 98

The term "panel composition" is somewhat tentative and is associated with the *germetch* whose pattern repeats the decoration of the *ensi's* lower panel. We may divide panel compositions into two basic types. The first, with its regular disposition of one or another secondary motif throughout the entire central field is characteristic of the *germetch*, the Tekke *mafrach*, the Salor *torba* with the *ovadan* design and the Arabatchi *asmalyk*. The second, with its rows of five or seven vertical figures reminiscent of plants disposed within the central field, is to be met in the decoration of the Yomud *asmalyk* and again on the Tekke *mafrach*.

pls. 42; 58, 59, 63; 12, 109

pls. 74–76; 60

In the second half of the nineteenth century there emerged new compositional arrangements borrowed either from decorative motifs of neighbouring peoples or from other types of items. Thus, Ersari carpets now had designs common to Afghan and Persian carpets or characteristic of Bukhara velvets. The Kazakhs, who started to make pile-woven carpets only towards the close of the nineteenth century, borrowed compositional arrangements from *chii* mats and felts. Especially diverse were the ornamental designs of Kirghiz *giliams*, some of which contained motifs borrowed from Kashgar and Khotan carpets: central field pattern with an unbroken floral design, etc. All this, together with a change in the proportions of the decorated surface as expressed in an increased border area, coupled with the diminution of the design and introduction of compositions of a nature alien to woven articles, considerably transformed the Central Asian carpet. Yet, even more significant changes in the last third of the nineteenth century were due to the rapid spread of synthetic dyes, which essentially worsened the colouring. The quality of the carpets also deteriorated as there was an inordinate increase in knot density, not accompanied by an uniform reduction of thickness of all the yarns in the fabric but resulting from vigorous beating down of the weft and pile, causing the carpets to lose their pliability and become hard and brittle.

The decline in carpet weaving which began towards the close of the nineteenth century was exacerbated during the First World War, when all the country's arts and crafts stagnated and the output of woven goods dropped as the former nomadic tribes became settled.

Soviet times introduced a new chapter in the making of rugs and carpets in the Central Asian republics. Since 1926 much has been done in Turkmenia to organize carpet weavers into cooperatives, ensure a steady market for them and provide them with the basic materials and dyes. In 1929, the cooperatives were reorganized into the Union of Carpet Makers of the Turkmen Soviet Socialist Republic. In 1963, all the related factories and workshops manufacturing hand-knotted carpets were brought under one roof by the formation of the *Turkmenkovior* (Turkmen Carpet) firm.

Though pile carpets continue to be made in traditional styles, today's designers and carpet weavers seek new forms of artistic expression, producing, for example, portrait and scenic carpets. Nevertheless the basic product of the Carpet Union and the *Turkmenkovior* firm remains the classical patterned carpet. Apart from mass-produced pieces, many unique carpets have been made for exhibitions and interior decoration of public buildings. Among these are the Tekke carpet which won a prize at the 1937 Paris World Fair, the *kejebe* and *darvaza gül* carpets (1947) and the curtain carpet for the Bolshoi Opera House in Moscow (1941). In technique and design these are in no way inferior to the finest of the older rugs and carpets and,

pl. 29

although vast in size, they manifest a correct proportion between the *göls*, central field and borders.

The efforts to promote the production of traditional Central Asian carpets encounter certain difficulties as the meaning of most motifs has been lost and only a new approach by artists and designers can help today to create a composition employing the old ornamental motifs. Only *göl* designs are utilized in modern woven articles. As a result of this one-sided attitude to the legacy of the Central Asian carpet, which looks back to the close of the nineteenth century, the compositional arrangements and designs of many carpet products of the past are no longer used at all. Today many people, even in Central Asia itself, are familiar only with main carpets; the smaller pieces have been undeservedly forgotten.

The objective of producing works of decorative and applied arts for modern residential and public interiors provides carpet-makers with considerable opportunities for creating a diverse range of products serving new functions.

It should be noted that today the art of carpet making continues also as a cottage industry. Thus the Turkomans living along the Caspian Coast and the Kirghiz resident in Ferghana Valley extensively practise the making of pile carpets and rugs both for their domestic needs and for the market. Despite marked changes, artistically these products still manifest local features and the technique is traditionally impeccable. Central Asian carpet weavers are proceeding with their search for innovation, while jealously preserving their superb, time-hallowed popular heritage.

[1] A. A. Bogolyubov, *Carpets of Central Asia*, St. Petersburg, 1908 (in Russian); A. A. Semionov, "Carpets of Russian Turkestan", *Ethnographical Review*, Nos. 1, 2, pp. 137–179, 1911 (in Russian); A. A. Felkerzam, "Old Carpets of Central Asia", *Old Years*, October–December 1914 (in Russian); S. M. Dudin, "Carpets of Central Asia", *Works of the Museum of Anthropology and Ethnography*, vol. VII, 1928 (in Russian).

[2] V. G. Moshkova, "Tribal Göls in Turkoman Carpets", *Soviet Ethnography*, vol. I, 1946 (in Russian; English translation in *Turkoman Studies I*, Ed. R. Pinner and H. Franses, London 1980); *idem, Carpets and Rugs of the People of Central Asia. Late 19th and Early 20th Century*, Tashkent, 1970 (in Russian).

[3] In the thirteenth and fourteenth centuries the Salor, Saryk, Tekke and Ersari were united in the Salor (Soinkhan) federation while the Chodor, Arabatchi and several other tribes were associated in the Chodor (Essenkhan) federation.

[4] K. Erdmann, *The History of the Early Turkish Carpet*, London, 1977.

GLOSSARY

Abr (throughout Central Asia), cloud motif

Ai, ai kochot (Kirghiz), moon motif

Aina (Turkoman), mirror motif

Aina gochak, aina kochak (Turkoman), mirror with horns motif

Aina khalta (Turkoman), small mirror bag

Aina khamtoz (Turkoman), stepped mirror motif

Ak (throughout Central Asia), white

Ak gyra (Turkoman), white band, white border motif

Ak su (Turkoman), white water motif

Ala, alajip, alaja (Turkoman), speckles, coloured strip

Ala govurdak (Turkoman), speckled bits of fried meat motif

Algam (Turkoman), meaning unknown

Arabatchi göl (Turkoman), main tribal *göl* of the Arabatchi Turkomans (see *göl*)

Asmalyk (Turkoman), twin flank trappings for a wedding camel

Atanak (Turkoman), cross motif, sometimes called *tekbent*

Ashyk (Turkoman), cube of small bones motif

Ayatlyk (Turkoman), funerary rug

Bashtyk (Kirghiz), tent bag

Baskur (Karakalpak, Kirghiz, Uzbek), broad tent band

Bodom (Turkoman, Uzbek), almond motif

Bovrek (Turkoman), bud motif

Bukhcha (Turkoman), book case

Buynuz (Turkoman), horn or horns motif

Chakmak (Turkoman), tinder, lightning motif

Charkh palak (Turkoman), cross, vault of sky motif, also called *sagdak gül*, the Sogdian motif

Chavadan (Kirghiz), kit bag

Chemche (Turkoman), spoon motif

Chetanak (Turkoman), lattice motif

Chii (throughout Central Asia), local rush-type plant and articles made of it

Chinakap (throughout Central Asia), bowl case

Chinar gül (Turkoman), plane-tree blossom

Choidysh (throughout Central Asia), teapot motif

Chodor göl (Turkoman), main tribal *göl* of the Chodor Turkomans (see *göl*)

Chodor muiiz (Karakalpak), Chodor horns motif

Chuval (Turkoman), tent bag

Chuval göl (Turkoman), *chuval* motif, also called *sary göl, maida göl, kichik göl*

Darak (Turkoman), comb motif

Darvaza gül (Turkoman), gates motif

Dezlik (Turkoman), a small tent door rug which also serves as the collar for the leading camel of a wedding caravan

Doga, dogajik, dogdan (throughout Central Asia), talisman motif

Dogry darak (Turkoman), straight comb motif

Duochitme (Turkoman), symmetrical knot

Dyrnak (Turkoman), claws motif

Dyrnak göl (Turkoman), one of the main *göls* of the Yomud Turkomans

Elem (Turkoman), additional panels or border in pile weavings

Ensi (Turkoman), tent-door hanging

Erik gül (Turkoman), apricot blossom motif

Erre (Turkoman), saw-like motif

Eshik tysh (Kirghiz), tent-door hanging

Eyerlik (Turkoman), saddlecloth

Gapyrga (Turkoman), ribs motif

Gara nagysh (Turkoman), black motif

Gaz ayak (Kirghiz, Turkoman), goose foot motif

Gelin barmak (Turkoman), married woman's fingers motif

Gerati (throughout Central Asia), Herati motif

Germetch (Turkoman), tent door threshold rug

Giliam (Kazakh, Kirghiz), main carpet

Girikh (throughout Central Asia), knot motif

Giyak (Turkoman), slanting motif

Gochak (Turkoman), scrolls or small horns motif

Göl (Turkoman), tribal emblem medallion used primarily to ornament main carpets

Gosha kelle (Turkoman), twinned heads motif

Govacha gül (Turkoman), cotton-boll motif

Govurdak (Turkoman), bits of fried meat motif

Gozenek (Turkoman), meaning unknown

Gujuk izy (Turkoman), trace of the puppy motif

Gül (Turkoman), pattern, flower motif

Gülli göl (Turkoman), one of the main *göls* of the Ersari Turkomans (see *göl*)

Gulyaidy (Turkoman), meaning unknown

Gurbaka (Kirghiz), frog motif

Gush, Kush (Turkoman), bird motif

Iashil su (Turkoman), green-water motif

Igsalik (Turkoman), spindle bag

Iirek (Kirghiz), uneven, curved motif

Ilmek (Kirghiz), hook motif

Iolam (Turkoman), tent band

Itik gül keleti (Turkoman), meaning unknown

It taman (Kirghiz), trace of the dog motif

Julkhyrs (Uzbek), literally 'bearskin', a type of high pile carpet

Kaikalak (Kirghiz), image, idol, or curved motif

Kalkan nuska (Nurata Uzbek), shield motif

Kap (throughout Central Asia), bag

Kapsa göl (Turkoman), main tribal *göl* of the Yomud Turkomans (see *göl*), literally lattice motif

Kapunuk (Turkoman), door surround

Karchin, karshin (throughout Central Asia), kit bag

Kejebe (Turkoman), wedding litter on the camel motif

Kelle (Turkoman), head motif

Kerege nuska (Kirghiz), *yurt* lattice motif

Khali (Turkoman), main carpet

Khalyk (Turkoman), see *dezlik*

Khamtoz (Turkoman), zigzag, stepped motif
Khurjin (Kirghiz, Uzbek, Karakalpak), saddlebag
Khurjun (Turkoman), saddlebad
Kilem (Kirghiz), carpet
Koinekche nagshy (Turkoman), scissors motif
Kojanak (Turkoman), carved, crooked, with horns motif
Kosh jabyk (Kirghiz), hanging cot
Kuchkor, kuchkorak (Kirghiz, Uzbek), ram motif
Kuchkor shokh (Uzbek), ram's horns motif
Kiyak (Kirghiz), slanting motif
Mafrach (Turkoman), small tent bag
Mary göl (Turkoman), see Salor *göl*
Mashaty (Kirghiz), meshed motif
Mihrab (throughout Central Asia), pointed arch
Muiiz (Kazakh, Karakalpak, Uzbek), horns motif
Muiuz (Kirghiz), horns motif
Naldag (Turkoman), horse shoe motif
Namazlyk (throughout Central Asia), prayer rug
Napramach (Uzbek), bag for household utensils
Ojakbashi (Turkoman), hearth surround rug
Ok gözi (throughout Central Asia), arrow point motif
Omurtka (Kirghiz), ribbed motif
Onurga (Turkoman), vertebrae motif
Orus kochot (Kirghiz), Russian design
Ovadan (Turkoman), flourishing, beautiful motif
Ovadan gyra (Turkoman), band with ovadan motif
Pakhta (Uzbek), cotton motif
Sainak (Turkoman), meaning unknown
Saldat (Turkoman), soldiers motif
Sallanchak (Turkoman), cot

Salor göl (Turkoman), main tribal *göl* of the Salor Turkomans, also known as Mary *göl*
Sarai kilem (Kirghiz), palace carpet (very large carpet)
Sarkhalka (Turkoman), earring motif
Sary göl (Turkoman), main tribal *göl* of the Saryk Turkomans
Sary gyra (Turkoman), yellow border motif
Sary ichyan (Turkoman), yellow scorpion motif
Sekiz keshde (Turkoman), eight drawings motif
Sekme gül (Turkoman), elongated flower motif
Shabadan (Kazakh), kit bag
Shemle (Turkoman), shawl motif
Sychan izy (Turkoman), mouse trail motif
Syngyrma (Turkoman), meaning unknown
Syrga (throughout Central Asia), meaning unknown
Tarak (Uzbek), comb motif
Tekbent (Turkoman), women's leather belt motif
Tekke göl (Turkoman), main tribal *göl* of the Tekke Turkomans (see *göl*)
Tengejik (Turkoman), small coin motif
Toguz dobo (Kirghiz), nine hillocks motif
Tomyzkhan gyra (Turkoman), meaning unknown
Torba (throughout Central Asia), kit bag
Tumar, tumarcha (throughout Central Asia), incense vessel motif
Umurtka (Kirghiz), vertebrae motif
Uriuk gül (Turkoman), apricot blossom motif
Uuk bash, uuk kap (throughout Central Asia), strut pole cover
Yarachitme (Turkoman), asymmetrical knot
Yulduz (Kirghiz), star motif

KEY TO STRUCTURE ANALYSES

S—plied in a clockwise direction.
Z—plied in an anti-clockwise direction.
The yarn structure is given in the following sequence:
(i) direction of spin of individual strands
(ii) number of strands in the yarn
(iii) direction of ply of the yarn
Examples: Z2S—yarn of two Z spun strands, plied S
Z2—yarn of two Z spun strands, unplied
Z1—yarn of one Z spun strand
Pile height was measured from the weft.

Knot density—number of knots in the direction of the weft multiplied by number of knots in the direction of the warp in one square decimetre. Given in parenthesis is the knot ratio.

Surface area data are presented as follows: in carpets, first length and then width; in hangings, first width and then height.

Finish (selvedges, upper end, lower end) is described from the direction of the article's function, not of weaving (for instance, there are pieces woven "upside down" or "sideways").

Wrapping—a method of finishing the selvedges when several edge warps are tightly oversewn.
Overcasting—a method of finishing the selvedges when two or more edge warps are simply interlaced. Usually thick yarns (some times of different colours) are employed: as a result the edge resembles a plaited band.
Plaiting—a method of finishing the selvedges when several edge warps are plaited to form a braid.
Salor *torbas* have been found to have two variations in the design of the lower *elem* panel. One is the *khamtoz*, the other has not been identified, which is why we have decided to call it "the second variation of the Salor *elem*".
The names of ornaments are, for the most part, those given by V. G. Moshkova, G. Saurova, K. I. Antipina and T. A. Zhdanko.
The map showing where the main groups of the different Turkmen tribes were located has been taken from: Ya. V. Vinnikov, *The Economy, Culture and Life of the Rural Population of the Turkmen SSR*, Moscow, 1969 (in Russian).

KEY TO ABBREVIATED LITERATURE

Antipina 1962 — K. I. Antipina, *Specific Features of the Material Culture and Art of the Southern Kirghiz*, Frunze, 1962 (in Russian)

Azadi 1975 — S. Azadi, *Turkoman Carpets and the Ethnographic Significance of Their Ornaments*, Fishguard, 1975

Benardout 1974 — R. B. Benardout, *Catalogue of Turkoman Weaving Including Beluch*, London, 1974

Beresneva 1976 — L. G. Beresneva, *The Decorative and Applied Art of Turkmenia*, Leningrad, 1976

Black, Loveless 1976 — *Rugs of the Wandering Baluchi* (compiled by D. Black and C. Loveless), London, 1976

Bogolyubov 1908 — A. A. Bogolyubov, *Carpets of Central Asia*, St. Petersburg, 1908 (in Russian)

Bogolyubov 1973 — A. A. Bogolyubov, *Carpets of Central Asia* (edited by J. M. A. Thompson), Wolverton, Basingstoke: Crosby Press, 1973

Denny 1979 — W. B. Denny, *Oriental Rugs*, Washington, D.C., 1979

Dimand, Mailey 1973 — M. S. Dimand, J. Mailey, *Oriental Rugs in the Metropolitan Museum of Art*, New York, 1973

The Ersari 1975 — *The Ersari and Their Weavings, Christmas Exhibition of the International Hajji Baba Society*, Washington, D.C., 1975

Felkerzam 1914 — A. A. Felkerzam, "Old Carpets of Central Asia", *Old Years*, October–December 1914 (in Russian)

Gombos 1975 — K. Gombos, *Régi Türkmén Szönyegek*, Budapest, 1975

Hali Vol. 1 (1978)—5 (1982) — The International Journal of Oriental Carpets and Textiles

Jones, Boucher 1973 — H. McCoy Jones and J. W. Boucher, *Tribal Rugs from Turkestan, Christmas Exhibition of the International Hajji Baba Society*, Washington, D.C., 1973

Mackie, Thompson 1980 — L. W. Mackie, J. Thompson, Ed., *Turkmen Tribal Carpets and Traditions*, Washington, D.C., 1980

McMullan, Reichert 1970 — J. V. McMullan, D. O. Reichert, *The George Walter Vincent and Belle Townsley Smith Collection of Islamic Rugs*, Springfield, 1970

Moshkova 1970 — V. G. Moshkova, *Carpets and Rugs of the Peoples of Central Asia. Late 19th and Early 20th Centuries*, Tashkent, 1970 (in Russian)

Pinner, Franses 1980 — R. Pinner and M. Franses, Ed., *Turkoman Studies I, Aspects of the Weaving and Decorative Arts of Central Asia*, London, 1980

Roberts 1981 — E. H. Roberts, *Treasures from Near Eastern Looms*, Brunswick, 1981

Saurova 1968 — G. Saurova, *The Turkmen Carpet of Today and Its Traditions*, Ashkhabad, 1968 (in Russian)

Thacher 1977 — A. B. Thacher, *Turkoman Rugs*, London, 1977

Transactions 1968 — *Transactions of the Kirghiz Archaeological and Ethnographical Expedition*, Vol. 5, Moscow, 1968 (in Russian)

1

Salor chuval

155×78 cm

18th century
Museum of Ethnography of the Peoples of
the USSR, Leningrad.[1] No. 87-24

Warp: ivory wool, Z2S.
Weft: two shoots, brown wool, Z2.
Pile: wool and silk, Z2S.
Knot: asymmetrical, open on left (ASIII), pile
turned upwards.
Knot density: 5,376 knots per dm^2 (1:1.3), pile
height 4 mm.
Dyes: natural.
Colours (nine): cherry-red, red-pink (similar to
ground), pink (silk), yellow, dark brown, dark blue,
sky-blue, dark green, ivory.
Finish: selvedges and ends cut and later wrapped
with blue wool.
Design and ornaments: rectangular central field
with three almost square Salor *göls* enclosing the
aina gochak motif, and with secondary *charkh palak*
ornaments; central field framed by three borders
with intermediate *alaja* stripes; main border decorated with the *kojanak* design, minor ones with the
chakmak motif; side *elem* panel undecorated, lower
elem panel carries fifteen vertical figures resembling
plants (top cut).
Published: Bogolyubov 1908, pl. 39.
Analogies: Jones, Boucher 1973, No. 20; Mackie,
Thompson 1980, ill. 8; Denny 1979, ill. 61.

---

[1] Further on: Museum of Ethnography, Leningrad

1

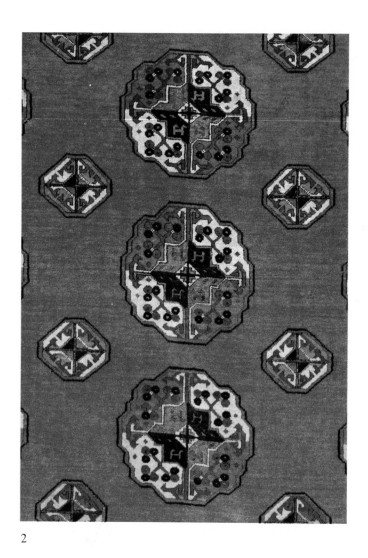

2

2, 3
Salor khali

270×380 cm

> 18th century
> The Hermitage, Leningrad. No. VT-754

Warp: grey wool, Z2S.
Weft: two shoots, lightly twisted, brown wool, Z2S.
Pile: wool, Z2S; silk, Z3S.
Knot: asymmetrical, open on left (ASIII).
Knot density: 2,552 knots per dm² (1:1.3), pile height 4 mm.
Dyes: natural.
Colours (nine): intensive red, violet-red, pink (wool and silk), orange-red, dark brown, salmon-pink, dark blue, sky-blue, white.
Finish: selvedges—six warp cables of three threads each, overcast with blue and red wool; ends missing.
Design and ornaments: rectangular central field with 6 by 13 rows of old Salor *göls* and secondary *chuval göls*; central field framed by three borders, with main one containing stylized unidentified design, reminiscent of Kufic inscription; minor ones carry the *tekbent* motif.
Published: *Culture and Art of the Peoples of the Soviet East. State Hermitage Room Guide* (in Russian). Leningrad, 1963, p. 75.
Analogies: Mackie, Thompson 1980, pls. 4, 5; Jones, Boucher 1973, No. 16.

4 →
Salor kapunuk

128×128 cm

> Late 18th or early 19th century
> Museum of Ethnography,
> Leningrad. No. 26-94

Warp: ivory wool, mixed with brown, Z2S.
Weft: two shoots, white wool, mixed with brown, Z2.
Pile: wool, Z2.
Knot: asymmetrical, open on left (ASIII).
Knot density: 3,285 knots per dm² (1:1.6); pile height 4 mm.
Dyes: natural.
Colours (nine): two shades of terracotta-red, orange, yellow, dark brown, dark blue, sky-blue, blue-green, ivory.
Finish: selvedges—terracotta-red wool, wrapped round three warps; upper end—2 cm red and white plain weave, folded back and sewn down; brown plaited band embroidered with silk and trimmed with orange wool; bottom transverse edge, similarly worked; lower end—originally warps ended in fringe knotted on four pairs of warps; 12 cm long fringe of green and pink silk, sewn later onto ends.

4

5

Design and ornaments: central field, repeating *kapunuk's* Π-shaped form filled with the *ovadan* motif; vertical bands flanking central field carry a variation of the *khamtoz* motif; transverse band consists of three borders; main one has a variation of the *erik gül* motif; design of minor ones has not been identified; upper narrow border decorated with the *gochak* motif.

Published: Felkerzam 1914, p. 101.

Analogies: Bogolyubov 1973, pl. 5 (central field motif); McMullan, Reichert 1970, pl. 69; Mackie, Thompson 1980, ill. 15.

5
Salor torba

127×42 cm

18th century
The Russian Museum, Leningrad.
No. KOB-215

Warp: ivory wool, Z2S.
Weft: two shoots, very fine, brown wool, Z2S.
Pile: wool and silk, Z2S.
Knot: asymmetrical, open on left (ASIII).
Knot density: 3,744 knots per dm^2 (1:1.5), pile height 3 mm.
Dyes: natural.
Colours (eight): cherry-red, violet-brown, pink (silk), dark brown, blue, sky-blue, blue-green, ivory.
Finish: selvedges and upper end cut and later wrapped with red wool; lower end—ivory plain weave, cut; 16 cm dark blue fringe, knotted on two pairs of warps.
Design and ornaments: rectangular central field with straight 7 by 2 lattice design filled with the *aina khamtoz* motif; framed by three borders; main one carries a variation of the *ashyk* motif; minor borders, the *ok gözi* motif; middle and intermediate stripes, the *alaja* motif; narrow side and upper *elem* panels undecorated; lower *elem* panel decorated with the *khamtoz* motif; top border carries the *gochak* motif.

First publication.

Analogies: Mackie, Thompson 1980, No. 12 (central field and broad border).

6
Salor chuval

132×85 cm

Late 18th century
Museum of Ethnography, Leningrad.
No. 26-79

Warp: ivory wool, Z2S.
Weft: two shoots, brown wool, Z2S.
Pile: wool and silk, Z2.
Knot: asymmetrical, open on left (ASIII).
Knot density: 3,675 knots per dm^2 (1:1.3); pile height 5 mm.
Dyes: natural.
Colours (twelve): two shades of light red, dark red, pinkish-red, violet-red, pink (silk), dark yellow, dark brown, dark blue, sky-blue, dark green, ivory.
Finish: selvedges missing; upper end—2 cm red and white plain weave, folded on face; red plaited band, sewn on; lower end missing.
Design and ornaments: rectangular central field with 4 by 4 rows of *sary göls* and secondary small octagonal *chuval göls*; central field framed by three borders, with main one carrying the *kojanak* motif and minor ones, the *chakmak* design; side and upper *elem* panels undecorated; lower *elem* panel contains four rows of small *kelle* designs; on top narrow border with unidentified design.

First publication.
Analogies: Beresneva 1976, pl. 15.

7
Salor chuval

132×85 cm

18th century
Museum of Ethnography, Leningrad.
No. 87-23

Warp: ivory wool, Z2S.
Weft: two shoots, brown wool, Z2S.
Pile: wool and silk, Z2S.
Knot: asymmetrical, open on left (ASIII).
Knot density: 2,552 knots per dm^2 (1:1.3), pile height 3.5 mm.
Dyes: natural.
Colours (twelve): cherry-red, purple-red, pinkish-red, pink (silk), orange, yellow, brown, violet-brown, blue, sky-blue, blue-green, ivory.
Finish: all edges cut and later wrapped with blue wool.
Design and ornaments: rectangular central field with 3 by 3 rows of tall *chuval göls* and secondary *chemche* figures (old Salor variant); central field framed by three borders with four intermediate *alaja* stripes; main border decorated with the *kojanak* motif and minor ones, with the *algam* motif; broad lower *elem* panel has sixteen figures reminiscent of trees.

First publication.
No near analogies identified.

6

7

8
Salor chuval

130×85 cm

Late 18th or early 19th century
Museum of Ethnography, Leningrad.
No. 26-32

Warp: white wool, mixed with grey, Z2S.
Weft: two shoots, dark brown wool, Z2S.
Pile: wool, Z2S.
Knot: asymmetrical, open on left (ASIII).
Knot density: 3,312 knots per dm^2 (1:1.6), pile height 3.5–4 mm.
Dyes: natural.
Colours (nine): dark red, bright red, violet-red, yellow, brown, dark blue, sky-blue, dark green, ivory.
Finish: selvedges—red wool, wrapped round four warps; upper end—white plain weave, folded over; red plaited band, sewn on top; blue woollen braided cord, woven in along edge; lower end missing.
Design and ornaments: rectangular central field with 4 by 4 rows of *sary göls* and secondary small octagonal *chuval göls*; central field framed by three borders and *alaja* intermediate stripes; main border carries the *kojanak* motif; minor ones, the *chakmak* design; *elem* panels undecorated; narrow border with unidentified geometrical design on top.

First publication.
Analogies: Mackie, Thompson 1980, pl. 7 (central field).

9
Salor chuval

124×81 cm

18th century
The Russian Museum, Leningrad.
No. KOB-202

Warp: ivory wool, Z2S.
Weft: two shoots, dark brown wool, Z2S.
Pile: wool and silk, Z2S.
Knot: asymmetrical, open on left (ASIII).
Knot density: 3,036 knots per dm^2 (1:1.4); pile height 4 mm.
Dyes: natural.
Colours (nine): cherry-red, violet-brown, pink (silk), orange, dark brown, dark blue, sky-blue, blue-green, ivory.
Finish: selvedges—three pairs of warps, overcast with cherry-red wool; upper end—on face 2 cm cherry-red plain weave, covered with pink plaited band; upper edge, oversewn with dark blue wool; on back 1 cm cherry-red plain weave, folded back and sewn down; lower end missing.
Design and ornaments: rectangular central field with 3 by 3 rows of *sary göls* and secondary design of the Salor variation of the *chemche* motif; central field framed by three borders; main one carries the *kojanak* design, minor ones contain the *chakmak* design; four intermediate borders carry the *alaja* motif; side and upper *elem* panels undecorated; lower *elem* panel has fourteen vertical figures reminiscent of plants; narrow border with geometrical ornament on top.

First publication.
No analogies identified.

8

9

10

11

10
Salor asmalyk

148×82.5 cm

Late 18th or early 19th century
Museum of Ethnography, Leningrad.
No. 26-19

Warp: ivory wool, Z2S.
Weft: two shoots, brown wool, Z2.
Pile: wool and silk, Z2S.
Knot: asymmetrical, open on left (ASIII).
Knot density: 2,816 knots per dm^2 (1:1.5); pile height 5 mm.
Dyes: natural.
Colours (eight): red, bright red, violet-red, orange, crimson (silk), brown, dark blue, ivory.
Finish: selvedges—red wool, wrapped round two warps; blue and red plaited band with tassels, sewn onto upper part midway down; upper end—dark blue and white plain weave, folded over on back and sewn down; lower end missing; 41 cm long dark blue fringe knotted on four warps.
Design and ornaments: octagonal T-shaped central field with large star-shaped rosette enclosing the *girikh* motif; flanked by smaller rosettes of simple outline; eight *kejebe* arches (four interconnected on either side) form secondary designs; central field framed by five borders; broad main border with the *ashyk* motif between two minor borders with the *chakmak* motif and guard borders with the *algam* motif; intermediate stripes carry the *alaja* motif; *elem* panel undecorated at top but with the *khamtoz* design at bottom and two thirds upwards along sides; top border decorated with the *gochak* motif.

Published: Felkerzam 1914, pp. 72–73.
Analogies: Gombos 1975, No. 37; Mackie, Thompson 1980, ill. 9, 14 (central field and border composition).

11
Salor torba

119×42.5 cm

Late 18th or early 19th century
Museum of Ethnography, Leningrad.
No. 87-16

Warp: ivory wool, Z2S.
Weft: two shoots, brown wool, Z2S.
Pile: wool and silk, Z2S.
Knot: asymmetrical, open on left (ASIII).
Knot density: 3,362 knots per dm^2 (1:2), pile height 3.5 mm.
Dyes: natural.
Colours (eight): red, terracotta-red, dark pink (silk), orange, brown, dark blue, dark green, ivory.
Finish: selvedges—wrapped with dark green wool; blue and red-orange plaited band, sewn on; upper end—red and white plain weave, folded back and sewn down; brownish woven band embroidered with silk; lower end missing; 40 cm long dark blue fringe, attached.
Design and ornaments: rectangular central field with diagonal *ak su* lattice design; framed by three borders; main one has a variant of the *gochak* motif, minor ones contain two rows of diamonds separated by slanted crosses (unidentified pattern); intermediate stripes carry the *alaja* motif; side and upper *elem* panels undecorated, lower one embellished with second variation of the Salor *torba elem*; top border decorated with the *gochak* motif.

Published: Bogolyubov 1908, pl. 9.
Analogies: Felkerzam 1914, pp. 72–73 (central field).

12
Salor torba

144×55 cm

Late 19th century
Museum of Ethnography, Leningrad.
No. 87-10

Warp: white wool, Z2S.
Weft: two shoots, very fine, light grey wool, Z2S.
Pile: wool, Z2S.
Knot: asymmetrical, open on left (ASIII).
Knot density: 2,418 knots per dm^2 (1:1.6), pile height 2 mm.
Dyes: natural and synthetic.
Colours (eight): brilliant red, violet-red, yellow, dark brown, dark blue, sky-blue, green-blue, white.
Finish: selvedges—three warps, oversewn with blue wool; upper end—1 cm brown plain weave and 0.5 cm brilliant-red plain weave, on face; 3 cm white plain weave, folded back and sewn down; lower end—2.5 cm white plain weave, folded over on back and sewn down; 53 cm long dark blue fringe on four warps, attached.
Design and ornaments: rectangular central field with the *ovadan* design; framed by three borders, broad main one with the *gochak* motif, minor ones with the *algam* motif, and intermediate stripes with the *alaja* motif; narrow side and top *elem* panels undecorated; lower *elem* panel carries the *khamtoz* motif; top border has the *gochak* and *ok gözi* motifs.

Apparently the *torba* was modelled on an older piece, cf. examples in the Bogolyubov collection, part of which is now in the Museum of Ethnography; V. G. Moshkova also had similar items in her collection, now in the Uzbek SSR State Museum of Art in Tashkent.

Published: Bogolyubov 1908, pl. 38.
No analogies identified.

12

13
Salor torba

116×41 cm

18th century
Museum of Ethnography, Leningrad.
No. 26-90

Warp: ivory wool, Z2S.
Weft: two shoots, brown wool, Z2S.
Pile: wool and silk, Z2S.
Knot: asymmetrical, open on left (ASIII).
Knot density: 3,929 knots per dm^2 (1:1.4); pile height 2 mm (heavily frayed).
Dyes: natural.
Colours (ten): dark brick-red, violet-red, bright red, pink (silk), crimson (silk), yellow, dark brown, dark blue, sky-blue, ivory.
Finish: selvedges—dark blue wool, wrapped round several warp cables; red and green plaited band, terminating in a loop; tassel, sewn on midway up the side; upper end—red and white plain weave, folded over on the front and sewn down; red and brown plaited band, embroidered with crimson silk; lower end missing; green, red and red-brown fringe, attached later.

Design and ornaments: rectangular central field with diagonal *shemle* lattice design; framed by three borders, with main one having the *ashyk* motif, minor ones the *algam* motif; intermediate stripes contain the *alaja* motif; side and upper *elem* panels undecorated; lower *elem* panel displays the *khamtoz* motif; top border decorated with the *gochak* motif.

Published: Felkerzam 1914, pp. 72–73.
Analogies: Jones, Boucher 1973, No. 13.

13

14

14
Salor torba

106×43 cm

Late 18th or early 19th century
Museum of Ethnography, Leningrad.
No. 87-8

Warp: ivory wool, Z2S.
Weft: two shoots, brown wool, lightly twisted, Z2S.
Pile: white, blue and some red wool, Z2S; other colours, Z2S; silk, Z3S, Z4S, Z2S.
Knot: asymmetrical, open on left (ASIII), pile turned upwards.
Knot density: 4,144 knots per dm² (1:1.3), pile height 2 mm.
Dyes: natural.
Colours (nine): cherry-red, violet-red, pink (silk), orange-red, dark brown, dark blue, sky-blue, blue-green, ivory.
Finish: selvedges—green wool, wrapped round four warps; upper end—1 cm red plain weave on face; 1 cm ivory plain weave, on back; lower end—ivory plain weave, folded over on back and sewn down; 19 cm long dark-blue fringe, knotted on four warps.

Design and ornaments: rectangular central field with diagonal *shemle* lattice pattern; framed by three borders, with main one having the *sekiz keshde* design; minor ones and intermediate stripes, the *alaja* motif; side and upper *elem* panels undecorated; lower *elem* panel embellished with second variation of the Salor *torba elem*; top border carries the *gochak* motif.

Published: Bogolyubov 1908, pl. 10.
Analogies: Pinner and Franses 1980, ill. 11 (central field and borders).

15

Saryk torba

126×40 cm

First half 19th century
Museum of Ethnography, Leningrad.
No. 37-13

Warp: ivory wool with some brown, Z2S.
Weft: two shoots, brown wool, lightly twisted, Z2S.
Pile: wool and cotton, lightly twisted, Z2S; silk, Z2.
Knot: symmetrical (SYI).
Knot density: 4,940 knots per dm^2 (1:1.9), pile height 2.5 mm.
Dyes: natural.
Colours (six): cherry-red, brilliant red, pink (silk), brown, dark blue, white (cotton).
Finish: selvedges—cherry-red wool, wrapped round several warp cables; upper end—blue and white plain weave; white plain weave, folded back and sewn down; lower end—blue and white plain weave, continues to form back of bag.

Design and ornaments: rectangular central field with row of six rosettes and five pairs of secondary *kejebe* arches with apexes facing one another; central field framed by three borders with main one carrying the *naldag* design and minor ones the *tekbent* motif; *elem* panels unpatterned; top border with the *sychan izy* motif.

First publication.
Analogies: Azadi 1975, pl. 31; Museum of Ethnography, Leningrad. No. 87-21.

15

16

16
Saryk ensi

160×116 cm

19th century
The Russian Museum, Leningrad.
No. KOB-158

Warp: ivory wool, tightly twisted, Z2S.
Weft: two shoots, brown wool, Z1.
Pile: wool, cotton, lightly twisted, Z2.
Knot: symmetrical (SYI)
Knot density: 3,040 knots per dm² (1:1.9), pile frayed.
Dyes: natural.
Colours (seven): cherry-red, crimson, orange, yellow, blue-green, mid-blue, white (cotton).
Finish: selvedges and ends cut; blue and red plaited band sewn on top later; blue wool wrapped round pile on right-hand side.
Design and ornaments: rectangular central field enclosed in four rows of U-shaped borders and divided into three panels along vertical axis, with pattern of top panel being mirror image of the bottom one, namely an axial arch formed by *algam* band enclosing the *kelle* motif; flanking the arch are rows of the *dogry darak* zoomorphic figures terminating at top with the *gochak* motif; central horizontal panel carries the *gaz ayak* design; first enclosing U-shaped border patterned on a version of the *darak* (?) motif; next broad border carries meander with the *gochak* motif separated by *khamtoz* stripe from broad band filled with the *gül* pattern; below is panel containing ten oblongs with the *dogry darak* design; lower border with the *gül* motif enclosed in narrow *khamtoz* stripes; base panel filled with the *itik gül keleti* pattern; entire composition is enclosed in a *khamtoz* border; borders, separated by narrow stripes, bear the *chetanak* motif.

First publication.
Analogies: see No. 17.

17 →
Saryk ensi

195×137 cm

19th century
Museum of Ethnography, Leningrad.
No. 87-3

Warp: ivory wool, Z2S.
Weft: two shoots, fine, brown wool, Z2S.
Pile: wool and cotton, Z2S.
Knot: symmetrical (SYI).
Knot density: 2,736 knots per dm² (1:2), pile height 5 mm.
Dyes: natural.
Colours (seven): red, orange, dark brown, olive-green, dark blue, green-blue, white (cotton).
Finish: brown wool, wrapped round two warps; upper end—2.5 cm grey plain weave, folded over on back and sewn down; on face, supplementary stitching with brown wool on two warps; lower end—12 cm olive-green plain weave; red-orange braided cord, woven in; striped plain weave, subsequently sewn on frayed fabric.
Design and ornaments: rectangular central field enclosed in four rows of U-shaped borders and divided along vertical axis into three panels, pattern of upper panel being mirror image of lower one, namely an axial arch formed by band with the *algam* pattern and central *kelle* motif; flanking the arch are rows of *dogry darak* zoomorphic figures terminating in the *gochak* motif; central horizontal panel carries the *gaz ayak* pattern; first U-shaped border enclosing central field carries axial row of pairs of bird's heads; next broad border filled with meander of *gochak* motifs and separated by narrow *khamtoz* stripe from broad band with the *gül* design; above this composition is panel consisting of seven arches on a ground with offset rows of coloured triangles and oblongs; lower panel has nine oblongs with the *dogry darak* design and separated by band with the *gül* motif from the base panel carrying the *itik gül keleti* pattern; the whole *ensi* framed by three borders with main one having the *sainak* motif and minor ones the *khamtoz* motif.

Published: Bogolyubov 1908, pl. 4.
Analogies: Thacher 1977, pl. 9; Dimand, Mailey 1973, pl. 247; Museum of Ethnography, Leningrad. No. 26-17.

17

18

← 18
Saryk ensi

147×165 cm

First half 19th century
The Russian Museum, Leningrad.
No. KOB-160

Warp: white and ivory wool, Z2S.
Weft: two shoots, brown wool, Z2S.
Pile: wool Z2S, cotton, Z3S, Z4S, silk, Z4S, Z5S.
Knot: symmetrical (SYII).
Knot density: 2,376 knots per dm^2 (1:1.8); pile height 2 mm (heavily frayed).
Dyes: natural.
Colours (seven): violet-red, orange, two shades of pink (wool and silk), brown, dark blue, white (cotton).
Finish: selvedges—eight pairs of warps, overcast with brown wool; upper end—4 cm brown plain weave, woven over two warps; lower end—6 cm brown plain weave; multi-coloured braided cord woven in, 3 cm away from pile.
Design and ornaments: rectangular central field framed by border with the *kelle* design (Saryk version); central section horizontally divided into three panels; design of upper panel being mirror image of lower one; axial arch (*algam*-motif version for *ensi*) with the kelle motif; flanking arch are rows of *dogry darak* zoomorphic figures, with the *gochak* design above; in the middle, horizontal panel has the *gaz ayak* pattern; three-panel composition enclosed in two U-shaped borders, geometrical motif of inner narrow border has not been identified; broad outer border carries meander pattern with three broad upright lines in the curves terminating in the *gochak* figures; above central field, enclosed in *kelle*-motif border, is four-arch panel, with spaces around and within the arches filled with diagonally arranged coloured triangles and oblongs; entire composition is enclosed by the *uriuk gül* pattern and by broad, U-shaped border with the *sainak* motif; lower part of the *ensi* has a "ground" panel with twin-row checkerboard *kelle* design in the Saryk version; narrow *khamtoz* border stripe frames the outside of the *ensi*.

First publication.
Analogies: Jones, Boucher 1973, No. 29; Thacher 1977, pl. 9, Pinner, Franses 1980, pl. 24 (central field and some borders).

19
Saryk kapunuk

119×83 cm

First half 19th century
Museum of Ethnography, Leningrad.
No. 87-9

Warp: white wool, lightly twisted, Z2S.
Weft: two shoots, fine, lightly twisted, light grey wool, Z2S.
Pile: wool and cotton, Z2S.
Knot: symmetrical (SYII), pile turned upwards.
Knot density: 2,520 knots per dm^2 (1:2), pile height 3 mm.
Dyes: natural.
Colours (seven): red magenta, orange, yellow, brown, dark blue, green, white (cotton).
Finish: selvedges—red-brown wool, wrapped round two pairs of warps on face; blue-green plaited band, sewn on above; couched in nine places by two thin twisted red cords, with paired red and green tassels; upper end—orange plain weave on face, 2 cm folded over on back and sewn down; green plaited band across the top; lower end—1.5 cm red plain weave followed by 50 cm of warps, wrapped (in groups of four), with wool of pile colours; small tassels.
Design and ornaments: Π-shaped central field with the *ovadan* meander pattern; framed by border with the *khamtoz* motif and undecorated intermediate stripe; top border carries the *gochak* motif.

Published: Bogolyubov 1908, pl. 5.
Analogies: Mackie, Thompson 1980, pl. 25.

20
Saryk torba

118×43 cm

19th century
The Russian Museum, Leningrad.
No. KOB-195

Warp: ivory wool, Z2S.
Weft: two shoots, red-dyed wool, Z2S.
Pile: wool and cotton, Z2S.
Knot: symmetrical (SYII), pile turned upwards.
Knot density: 3,120 knots per dm^2 (1:1.9), pile height 3 mm.
Dyes: natural.
Colours (eight): cherry-red, orange, crimson, brown, mid-blue, blue-green, yellow, white (cotton).
Finish: selvedges—red wool, wrapped round two pairs of warps; upper end—1.2 cm blue-green plain weave followed by 0.5 cm red plain weave, on face; 2.3 cm white fabric on back; lower end—ivory plain weave, cut; blue fringe knotted on warps, attached.
Design and ornaments: rectangular central field with 2 by 3 rows of *sary göls* and secondary *chemche* designs; central field framed by three borders, with main one carrying unidentified motif, and minor ones the *gozenek* design; intermediate borders carry the *alaja* motif; *elem* panels have small *doga* figures.

First publication.
Analogies: Mackie, Thompson 1980, No. 64.

21
Saryk torba

139×47 cm

First half 19th century
Museum of Ethnography, Leningrad.
No. 26-28

Warp: ivory wool, Z2S.
Weft: two shoots, light brown wool, Z2.
Pile: wool and silk, Z2, cotton, Z2S.
Knot: symmetrical (SYI).
Knot density: 3,008 knots per dm^2 (1:4), pile height 3 mm (frayed).
Dyes: natural.
Colours (eight): cherry-red, pink (silk), red (silk), orange, brown, dark blue, dark green, white (cotton).
Finish: selvedges—red wool, wrapped round several warp cables; upper end—red and white plain weave, folded over on back and sewn down; lower end— blue and white plain weave, partly cut; 17 cm long blue and red fringe, attached.
Design and ornaments: rectangular central field with 5 by 4 rows of small *sary göls* and secondary *chemche* designs; central field framed by three borders with two undecorated intermediate stripes; main border filled with the *naldag* pattern and minor ones, with the *gozenek* motif; undecorated *elem* panels; top border with *sychan izy* motif.

First publication.
Analogies: Turkmen SSR Museum of Arts, No. KII-2105 K-306; The Russian Museum, Leningrad. No. KOB-220.

20

21

22
Saryk chuval

140×90 cm

First half 19th century
The Russian Museum, Leningrad.
No. KOB-183

Warp: ivory wool, Z2S.
Weft: two shoots, lightly twisted, fine, brown wool
with some white, Z2.
Pile: wool, silk, cotton, lightly twisted, Z2S.
Knot: symmetrical (SYII).
Knot density: 4,250 knots per dm^2 (1:1.7); pile
height 3 mm.
Dyes: natural.
Colours (ten): cherry-red, crimson-red, pink (silk),
yellow, light yellow (silk), brown, dark blue, sky-
blue (silk), dark blue-green, white (cotton).
Finish: selvedges—cut and later wrapped with red
wool; upper end—2 cm red plain weave on face;
2 cm similar fabric, folded over on back and sewn
down; lower end—2 cm red plain weave, one strand
of blue thread; lower down ivory fabric, partly cut.
Design and ornaments: rectangular central field with
3 by 4 rows of *sary göls* and secondary *chemche*
designs; central field framed by three borders with

main one decorated with the *kojanak* design, minor
ones, with the *gozenek* design; intermediate borders
have the *chetanak* motif; narrow side *elem* panel
undecorated, upper and lower *elem* panels carry the
kelle motif; unpatterned blue border on top.

First publication.
Analogies: see No. 23.

22

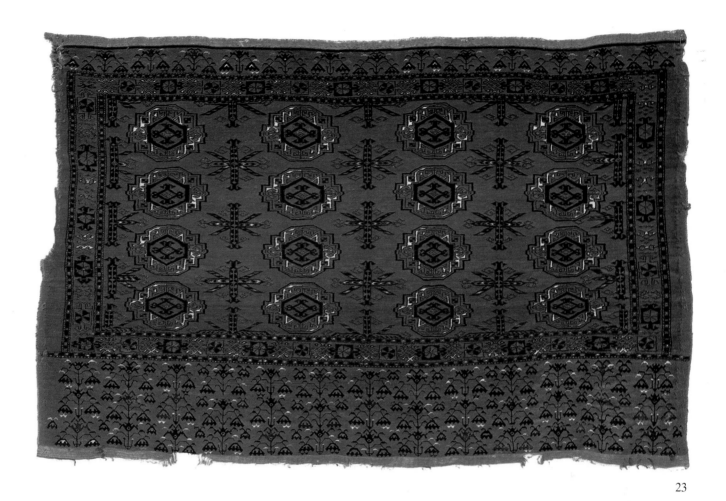

23

23
Saryk chuval

140×91 cm

First half 19th century
Museum of Ethnography, Leningrad.
No. 26-31

Warp: ivory wool, Z2S.
Weft: two shoots, brown wool, lightly twisted, Z2S.
Pile: wool and cotton, Z2S, silk, Z2.
Knot: symmetrical (SYI).
Knot density: 3,680 knots per dm^2 (1:1.8), pile height 4–5 mm.
Dyes: natural.
Colours (ten): red, brilliant red, orange, pink (silk), yellow, brown, dark blue, sky-blue, dark blue-green, white (cotton).
Finish: selvedges—red wool, wrapped round two warps; upper end—red and white plain weave, folded back and sewn down; lower end missing.
Design and ornaments: rectangular central field with 4 by 4 rows of *sary göls* and secondary *chemche* designs; central field framed by three borders with main one having the *kojanak* pattern, minor ones carrying unidentified geometrical ornament; inter-mediate borders contain the *alaja* motif; side *elem* panel undecorated, upper and lower *elem* panels decorated with the *kelle* design; unpatterned blue border on top.

First publication.
Analogies: Museum of Ethnography, Leningrad. Nos. 87-30 and 4493-9/1.2; The Russian Museum, No. KOB-183.

24

24
Saryk chuval

132×88 cm

Late 18th or early 19th century
Museum of Ethnography, Leningrad.
No. 26-75

Warp: ivory wool, Z2S.
Weft: two shoots, grey and brown wool, lightly twisted, Z2S.
Pile: wool and silk, lightly twisted, Z2S.
Knot: symmetrical (SYI).
Knot density: 3,500 knots per dm^2 (1:1.4), pile height 3 mm.
Dyes: natural.
Colours (nine): cherry-red, red, pink (wool and silk), flesh pink, dark yellow, brown, dark blue, dark green, white (cotton).
Finish: selvedges and lower end missing; upper end—ivory plain weave, folded over on back and sewn down.
Design and ornaments: rectangular central field with two large Mary *göls* enclosing the *aina gochak* pattern; secondary ornament, less complex version of the Mary *göl*; central field framed by three borders with two intermediate undecorated stripes; main border carries the *naldag* motif, minor borders, the *gozenek* design; upper *elem* panel undecorated, lower *elem* panel carries offset rows of small *kelle* motifs; top narrow border decorated with the *sychan izy* design.

First publication.
No analogies identified.

25
Saryk chuval

139×95 cm

Mid-19th century
Museum of Ethnography, Leningrad.
No. 26-96

Warp: ivory wool, Z2S.
Weft: two shoots, light brown wool, Z2S.
Pile: wool and cotton, Z2, silk, Z2S.
Knot: symmetrical (SYI).
Knot density: 3,577 knots per dm^2 (1:1.5), pile height 3.3–3.5 mm.
Dyes: natural.
Colours (seven): cherry-red, pink (silk), light pink (silk), yellow, brown, dark blue, white (cotton).
Finish: selvedges—cherry-red wool, wrapped round two warps; upper end—white plain weave, folded over and sewn down; lower end—white plain weave, folded over and sewn down.
Design and ornaments: rectangular central field with three Mary *göls* enclosing *chuval göls* and secondary *sary göls*; central field framed by three borders with two intermediate undecorated stripes; main border decorated with a version of the *kojanak* design and minor ones with the *tengejik* design; side narrow *elem* panel undecorated, upper and lower *elem* panels carry different versions of the *kelle* motif; top border contains the *giyak* motif.

First publication.
Analogies: Mackie, Thompson 1980, No. 22 (central field).

25

26
Saryk torba

115×47 cm

First half 19th century
The Russian Museum, Leningrad.
No. KOB-193

Warp: ivory wool, Z2S.
Weft: two shoots, dark brown wool, Z2S.
Pile: wool, cotton, Z2S, silk, Z2.
Knot: symmetrical (SYII).
Knot density: 3,259 knots per dm^2 (1:1.9), pile height 5 mm.
Dyes: natural.
Colours (seven): cherry-red, crimson (silk), orange, olive-brown, dark blue, green, white (cotton).
Finish: selvedges—cherry-red wool wrapped round two warps; upper end—red (0.5 cm) and ivory (2 cm) plain weave, folded over on back and sewn down; lower end cut; remains of dark blue fringe, knotted on two pairs of warps.
Design and ornaments: rectangular central field with 4 by 3 rows of *sekiz keshde* medallions and small *chuval göls* as secondary ornament; central field framed by three borders with main one decorated with a version of the *tomyzkhan gyra* (?) motif and minor ones with the *alaja* motif; round undecorated *elem* panel; top border with the *alaja* motif.

First publication.
No analogies identified.

27
Saryk torba

110×33 cm

18th century
Museum of Ethnography, Leningrad.
No. 26-27

Warp: ivory wool, lightly twisted, Z2S.
Weft: two shoots, brown wool, Z2.
Pile: wool, Z2S.
Knot: symmetrical (SYII).
Knot density: 4,223 knots per dm^2 (1:2.5), pile height 3.5 mm.
Dyes: natural.
Colours (seven): cherry-red, orange, olive-brown, mid-blue, sky-blue, green, ivory.
Finish: selvedges—red and brown wool, wrapped round three pairs of warps; upper end—red and ivory plain weave, folded over on back and sewn down; lower end—ivory plain weave, cut; remains of speckled fringe of pile colours; 22 cm long fringe, attached later.
Design and ornaments: rectangular central field with 3 by 2 rows of horizontally elongated unidentified 16-sided *göls*, and secondary *chemche* ornament; central field framed by three borders with main one carrying the *kojanak* motif and minor ones, the *giyak* design; undecorated *elem* panels; top narrow border with the *ala govurdak* motif.

First publication.
Analogies: Thacher 1977, table 22.

26

27

28
Tekke khali (fragment)

98×68 cm

18th century
The Russian Museum, Leningrad.
No. KOB-204

Warp: ivory wool, Z2S.
Weft: two shoots, very fine, white and red-dyed wool, Z2S.
Pile: wool, Z2S.
Knot: asymmetrical, open on right (ASII), with three end rows of symmetrical knots.
Knot density: 1,944 knots per dm^2 (1:1.6), pile height 2 mm (frayed).
Dyes: natural.
Colours (seven): violet-red, orange, brown, dark blue, sky-blue, green, ivory.
Finish: selvedges—blue wool, wrapped round two pairs of warps; ends missing.
Design and ornaments: rectangular central field with rows of Tekke *göls* and secondary *chemche* design; central field framed by three borders with main one carrying the *uriuk gül* motif, and minor ones, a version of the *gochak* design; intermediate borders contain the *giyak* motif; end *elem* panel with a version of the *gapyrga* design.

First publication.
No near analogies identified.

28

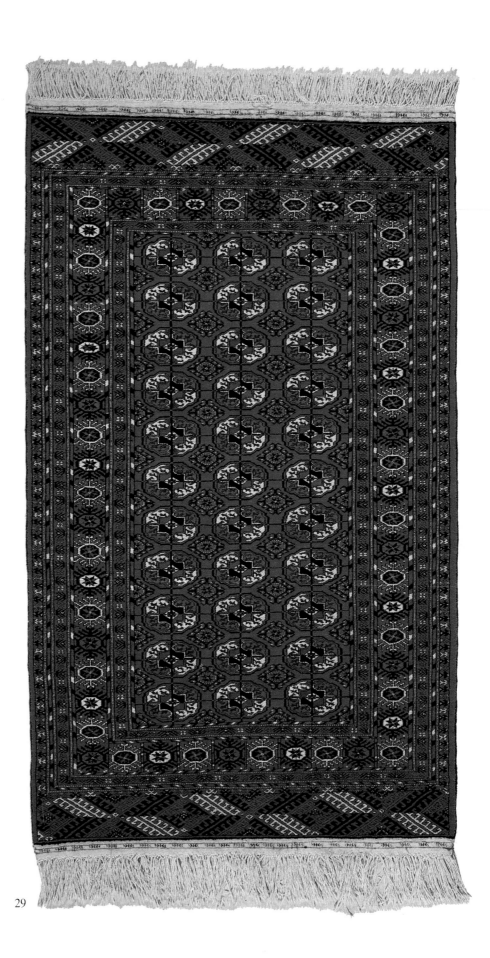

29

29
Turkoman khali

218×283 cm

1970s
Museum of Ethnography, Leningrad.
No. 9983-20

Warp: white wool, Z2S.
Weft: one shoot, white wool with some grey and brown, Z2S.
Pile: wool, lightly twisted, Z2S.
Knot: asymmetrical, open on right (ASII).
Knot density: 2,940 knots per dm^2 (1:1.8), pile height 5 mm.
Dyes: synthetic.
Colours (seven): crimson-red, pink, orange, mid-blue, blue-green, mid-green, white.
Finish: selvedges—blue wool, wrapped round three warps; ends—5 cm white plain weave with decorated woven stripe; warps end in fringe.
Design and ornaments: rectangular central field with 3 by 11 rows of Tekke *göls* and secondary diamond-shaped medallions with the *gochak* horns design; central field framed by four borders and eight intermediate stripes; main one carries the *uriuk gül* design, minor ones the *gochak* design (decoration of one minor border unidentified) and intermediate stripes the *gozenek* motif; *elem* panels on shorter sides decorated with a version of the *dyrnak* design. Hand-woven mass production.
First publication.

30 →
Tekke khali

152×109 cm

Last third 19th century
Museum of Ethnography, Leningrad.
No. 1166-1

Warp: white wool, Z2S.
Weft: two shoots, very fine, brown wool, mixed with grey, Z2S.
Pile: wool, Z2S.
Knot: asymmetrical, open on right (ASII).
Knot density: 3,648 knots per dm^2 (1:1.6), pile height 3 mm.
Dyes: natural and synthetic.
Colours (ten): brick-red, crimson, pink, orange, yellow, brown, dark blue, sky-blue, green, white.
Finish: selvedges—blue wool, wrapped round three warps; ends—6 cm white plain weave with red stripe; warps end in 8 cm long fringe.
Design and ornaments: rectangular central field contains straight *aina* lattice design and dividing bands with the *tekbent* pattern; central field framed by seven borders, with chain of white edged diamonds on main one and the *gelin barmak* and *tekbent* motifs on minor ones; ends have decorated *elem* panels consisting of straight lattice design with alternating motifs of oblongs and triangles.

First publication.
No near analogies identified.

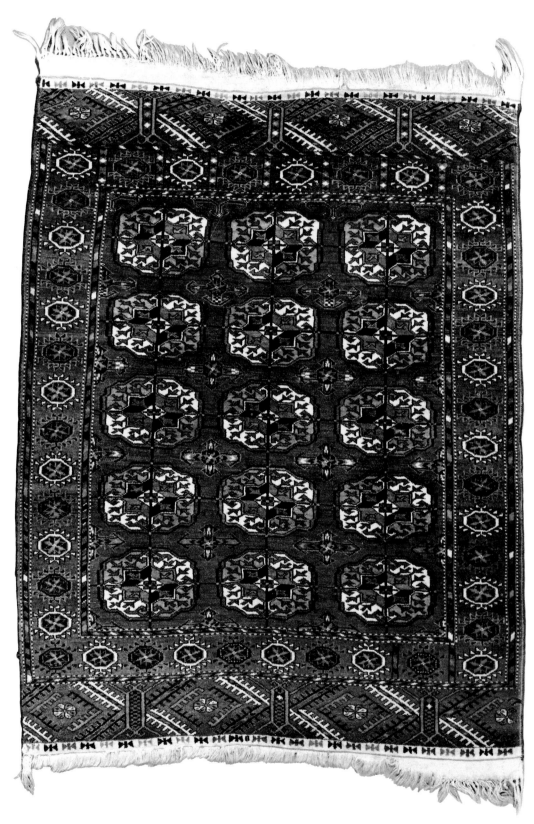

31

← 31
Tekke khali

125×100 cm

> 19th century
> Museum of Ethnography, Leningrad.
> No. 26-84

Warp: ivory wool, Z2S.
Weft: two shoots, brown wool, mixed with grey, Z2S.
Pile: wool, Z2S.
Knot: asymmetrical, open on right (ASII).
Knot density: 2,040 knots per dm^2 (1:1.8), pile height 4 mm.
Dyes: natural.
Colours (seven): dull red, orange, brown, dark blue, sky-blue, green, white.
Finish: selvedges—blue wool, wrapped round two pairs of warps; upper end—5 cm white plain weave with red stripe; warps (knotted in groups of six) end in fringe; lower end—finished similarly.
Design and ornaments: rectangular central field with 3 by 4 rows of Tekke *göls* and secondary *chemche* designs; central field framed by three borders with main one decorated with the *uriuk gül* design and minor ones with the *giyak* motif; at either end *elem* panel with the *dogdan* ornament.

First publication.
No near analogies identified.

32

32
Tekke khali (fragment)

167×76 cm

18th century
The Russian Museum, Leningrad.
No. KOB-176

Warp: ivory wool, Z2S.
Weft: two shoots, very fine, ivory wool with some brown and red-dyed wool, Z2S.
Pile: wool, Z2S.
Knot: asymmetrical, open on right (ASII), with three end rows of symmetrical knots.
Knot density: 2,176 knots per dm² (1:1.9), pile height 3 mm.
Dyes: natural.
Colours (seven): dark red, orange, brown, dark blue, green, ivory, white.
Finish: selvedges—blue wool, wrapped round two pairs of warps; lower end—0.5 cm red plain weave followed by green stripe; remainder missing.
Design and ornaments: rectangular central field with rows of Tekke *göls* (of which four are transverse), and secondary *chemche* design; central field framed by three borders with main one decorated with the *ovadan gyra* design, and minor ones with unidentified ornament of small diamonds and triangles.

First publication.
No near analogies identified.

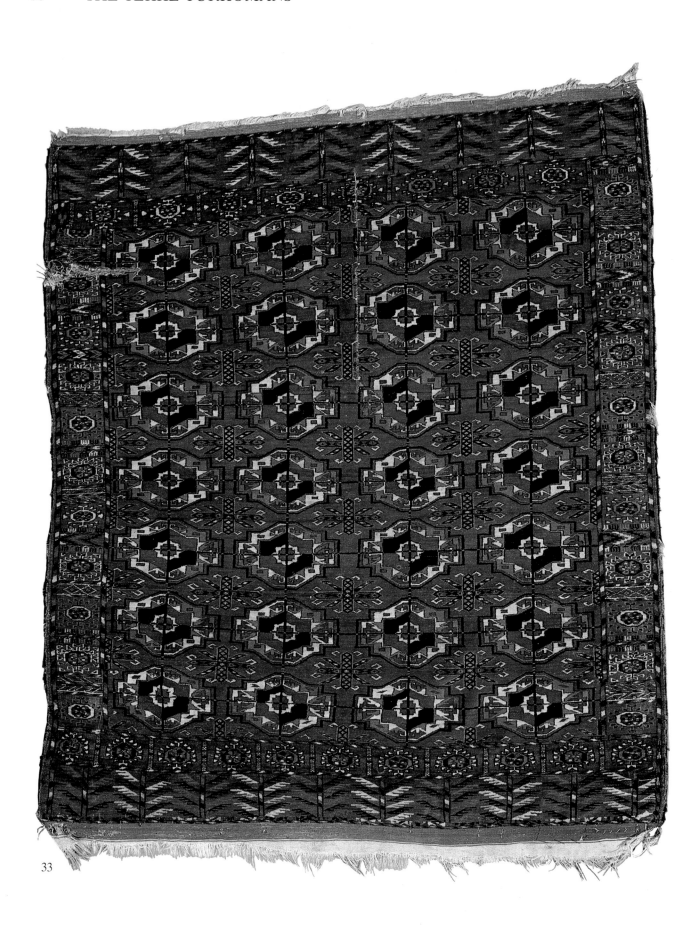

33

33
Tekke khali

136×117 cm

19th century
The Russian Museum, Leningrad.
No. KOB-192

Warp: ivory wool, Z2S.
Weft: one shoot, grey wool, mixed with white, Z2S.
Pile: wool, Z2S.
Knot: asymmetrical open on right (ASII), with four end rows of symmetrical knots.
Knot density: 2,880 knots per dm^2 (1:1.7), pile height 3 mm.
Dyes: natural.
Colours (six): violet-red, orange, dark brown, dark blue, sky-blue, ivory.
Finish: selvedges—blue wool, wrapped round two warps; ends—3 cm red and ivory plain weave; warps end in fringe.
Design and ornaments: rectangular central field with 4 by 7 rows of *chuval göls* and secondary *chemche* designs; central field framed by three borders with main one containing the *uriuk gül* design and minor ones the *gozenek* motif; flanked by *elem* panels carrying the *gapyrga* design.

First publication.
No near analogies identified.

34 →
Tekke ensi

150×107 cm

Last quarter 19th century
Museum of Ethnography, Leningrad.
No. 37-19

Warp: white wool, Z2S.
Weft: two shoots, with one strand of white wool, mixed with some grey and second strand of red-dyed wool, Z1.
Pile: wool, Z2S.
Knot: asymmetrical, open on right (ASII).
Knot density: 3,040 knots per dm^2 (1:1.9), pile height 3.5 mm.
Dyes: natural and synthetic.
Colours (seven): magenta red, red, brilliant red, brown, dark blue, green, white.
Finish: selvedges—blue wool, wrapped round three pairs of warps; upper end—1.8 cm white plain weave, folded over on back and sewn down; 27 cm long loops of red and white cotton threads, attached to corners; lower end—5 cm white plain weave with red stripe on three weft threads; warps end in tassels.
Design and ornaments: rectangular central field divided into three panels along vertical axis; decoration of upper panel is mirror image of lower one, with axial arch in the middle, formed of band with the *bovrek* pattern and filled with row of octagons, each enclosing the *dogajik* motif; arch flanked by oblongs containing the *gush* pattern; central horizontal panel decorated with the *govacha gül* design separated by horizontal bands with the *dogajik* motif; central field framed by three borders with main one decorated with a version of the *dogajik* design and minor ones with the *gozenek* design; upper transverse band intercepted in the middle by *mihrab* arch flanked by straight lattice designs of oblongs and triangles; overall composition framed by extremely broad band decorated with a variation of the *kelle* motif; borders decorated with the *sainak* motif run along edges and top; base panel carries small geometrical design.

First publication.
Analogies: Beresneva 1976, pl. 33.

34

35

← 35
Tekke ensi

183×133 cm

Second half 19th century
Museum of Ethnography, Leningrad.
No. 26-41

Warp: white wool, mixed with grey, Z2S.
Weft: two shoots, brown wool, Z2S.
Pile: wool, Z2S.
Knot: asymmetrical open on right (ASII).
Knot density: 1,980 knots per dm^2 (1:2.2), pile height 4 mm.
Dyes: natural.
Colours (seven): violet-red, crimson, yellow, dark brown, dark green, light green, white.
Finish: selvedges—end cable of warps, wrapped with red-orange wool; three pairs of warps, overcast with blue wool; upper end—6.5 cm plain weave with stripes of pile colours; in corners small angularly disposed rectangles; warp ends plaited into 55 cm long cord; lower end—plain weave similarly trimmed; warps end in 14 cm long fringe.
Design and ornaments: rectangular central field with the *gapyrga* decoration framed by three borders with main one carrying the *ovadan gyra* design and minor ones with the *koinekche nagshy* motif; base panel carries the *kelle* motif; entire composition enclosed within border carrying the *ok gözi* motif; top panel decorated with a version of the *gapyrga* motif.

First publication.
No near analogies identified.

36
Tekke kapunuk

104×76 cm

19th century
The Russian Museum, Leningrad.
No. KOB-163

Warp: white wool, Z2S.
Weft: two shoots, very fine, brown wool, Z2S.
Pile: wool, Z2S.
Knot: asymmetrical, open on right (ASII), pile turned upwards.
Knot density: 3,192 knots per dm^2 (1:2.1), pile height 3 mm.
Dyes: natural.
Colours (seven): brick-red, violet-red, brown, orange-red, dark blue, sky-blue, white.
Finish: selvedges—green wool, wrapped round two warps; upper end—blue-green plain weave, on face; white plain weave, on back, folded over and sewn down; orange-blue strip, stitched on face; braided orange-red strings, attached to corners; lower end—transverse strip of red plain weave, on face; white plain weave, on back, folded over and sewn down; multi-coloured woollen fringe of pile colours, attached; vertical stripes terminate at corners; white plain weave running along edge, folded over on back and sewn down; multi-coloured fringe, attached.
Design and ornaments: Π-shaped central field with the *dogajik* meander framed by two borders; outer one decorated with the *khamtoz* ornament and inner one with unidentified geometrical crosslike design; in lower corners both borders change to a diamond design; top border carries the *gochak* motif.

First publication.
Analogies: Mackie, Thompson 1980, pl. 46.

36

37

37, 38
Tekke kapunuk

109×77 cm

First half 19th century
Museum of Ethnography, Leningrad.
No. 26-54

Warp: ivory wool, mixed with brown and grey, Z2S.
Weft: two shoots, brown wool, mixed with some grey, Z1.
Pile: wool, Z2; silk, Z1.
Knot: asymmetrical, open on right (ASII), pile turned upwards.
Knot density: 4,062 knots per dm^2 (1:2.1), pile height 4 mm.
Dyes: natural.
Colours (ten): terracotta-red, bright red, pink (silk), orange, yellow, brown, mid-blue, sky-blue, blue-green, ivory.
Finish: selvedges—blue and blue-green wool, wrapped round two warps; upper end—2 cm red and white plain weave, folded over on back and sewn down; lower end—red plain weave, folded over on back and sewn down; multi-coloured 30 cm long fringe knotted on four warps; strings braided of red and blue woollen threads, attached to upper corners.
Design and ornaments: central Π-shaped field with the *dogajik* meander framed by several borders; vertical bands decorated with the *khamtoz* design, side bands undecorated; of three horizontal bands central one decorated with the *khamtoz* motif; band surrounding central field carries unidentified geometrical design; outer horizontal band contains the *syngyrma* and *gochak* designs on top and the *syngyrma* design below.

First publication.

Analogies: Felkerzam 1914, pp. 100–101 (central field).

38

39

39
Tekke dezlik

65×45 cm

19th century
Museum of Ethnography, Leningrad.
No. 26-49

Warp: ivory wool, Z2S.
Weft: one shoot, brown and light grey wool, Z1.
Pile: wool, Z2.
Knot: asymmetrical, open on right (ASII), pile turned upwards.
Knot density: 3,612 knots per dm^2 (1:2), pile height 2 mm.
Dyes: natural.
Colours (eight): dark red, orange-red, yellow-brown, mid-blue, two shades of sky-blue, green, ivory.
Finish: selvedges—green wool, wrapped round two pairs of warps; red and orange plaited band, attached to side; at top band ends in strings with tassels; upper end—red and white plain weave, folded over on back and sewn down; lower end—plain weave similarly finished; 40 and 50 cm long fringes, attached; upper part of fringe wrapped round with multi-coloured wool to form laces (evidently, original fringe was all wrapped).
Design and ornaments: Π-shaped central field with the *gochak* decoration on vertical bands and the *iashil su* motif on transverse band; framed by five borders with two unpatterned intermediate stripes; outer border carries the *tengejik* design, decoration of the next band unidentified; main border contains the *ak su* motif, and two borders flanking it carry the *giyak* design; *elem* panels, undecorated; top border carries the *alaja* motif.

First publication.
Analogies: Felkerzam 1914, pp. 44–45; Pinner, Franses 1980, pl. XXIV.

40 →
Tekke dezlik

78×47 cm

19th century
Museum of Ethnography, Leningrad.
No. 26-50

Warp: ivory wool, mixed with brown, Z2S.
Weft: one shoot, grey and brown wool, Z1.
Pile: wool, Z2.
Knot: asymmetrical, open on right (ASII), pile turned upwards.
Knot density: 4,928 knots per dm^2 (1:2.5), pile height 2.5 mm.
Dyes: natural.
Colours (seven): cherry-red, brilliant red, yellow, brown, dark blue, bluish-green, ivory.
Finish: selvedges—red wool, wrapped round warp cables; orange, red and blue braided cord, attached to side; upper end—3 cm red and white plain weave, folded over on back and sewn down; lower end—1.5 cm white plain weave, folded over on back and sewn down; wool of pile colours, wrapped round warp ends to form laces.
Design and ornaments: Π-shaped central field with the *gochak* motif on vertical bands and the *iashil su* motif on transverse band; framed by four borders and intermediate stripes undecorated and with the *alaja* pattern; main border with the *ak su* pattern flanked by the *giyak* stripes; inner narrow border with the *saldat* motif flanked by two *alaja* stripes; *elem* panels, undecorated; top stripe carries the *alaja* motif.

First publication.
Analogies: see No. 39.

40

41

← 41
Tekke dezlik

70×44 cm

Second half 19th century
The Russian Museum, Leningrad.
No. KOB-177

Warp: ivory wool, Z2S.
Weft: one shoot, brown wool, Z2S.
Pile: wool, Z2S.
Knot: asymmetrical, open on right (ASII), pile turned upwards.
Knot density: 4,224 knots per dm² (1:1.8), pile height 3 mm.
Dyes: natural and synthetic.
Colours (eight): red, bright red, orange, yellow, dark brown, dark blue, blue-green, white.
Finish: selvedges—sky-blue wool, wrapped round two warps; upper end—1 cm red plain weave, folded over on front; red and green plaited band, attached, long strings; lower end—1 cm white plain weave, folded over on back and sewn down; multi-coloured 57 cm long fringe knotted on four warps.
Design and ornaments: Π-shaped central field with the *kojanak* design on vertical bands and the *gochak* motif on transverse band; framed by three borders with the design of main one unidentified; minor borders display the *saldat* motif; *elem* panels, undecorated; top border carries geometrical design.

First publication.
Analogies: Pinner, Franses 1980, pp. 194, 396 (central field).

42

42
Tekke germetch

76×23 cm

19th century
The Russian Museum, Leningrad.
No. KOB-180

Warp: ivory wool, Z2S.
Weft: one shoot, very fine, white wool, mixed with grey, lightly twisted, Z2S.
Pile: wool and silk, Z2S.
Knot: asymmetrical, open on right (ASIII).
Knot density: 4,508 knots per dm² (1:2), pile height 2 mm.
Dyes: natural.
Colours (nine): bright red, pink (silk), orange, yellow, dark brown, dark blue, sky-blue, green, white.
Finish: selvedges—dark blue wool, wrapped round three warps; upper end—ivory plain weave, folded over on back and sewn down; edge oversewn with thick woollen threads, strings; lower end—ivory plain weave with embroidered band, carrying three rows of diamonds; arranged in checkered pattern between two red stripes; warps end in tassels.
Design and ornaments: rectangular central field with the *kelle* design framed by three borders with main one containing the *sainak* motif and minor ones the *gozenek* design; upper and narrow side *elems* undecorated; lower end has lattice design of 5 squares; at intersections minute crosses alternate with diamond-shaped figures.

First publication.
No near analogies identified.

43
Tekke asmalyk

140×83 cm

Late 18th or early 19th century
Museum of Ethnography, Leningrad.
No. 26-53/1

Warp: ivory wool, Z2S.
Weft: two shoots, camel hair, Z2.
Pile: wool, Z2S.
Knot: asymmetrical, open on right (ASII), with end row of symmetrical knots.
Knot density: 3,053 knots per dm^2 (1:1.7), pile height 2 mm.
Dyes: natural.
Colours (seven): dark red, bright red, orange-red, brown, mid-blue, sky-blue, white.
Finish: selvedges—red wool, wrapped round three warps; upper end—white plain weave, folded over on back and sewn down; lower end—2 cm white plain weave, folded over on back and sewn down; woven ornamented band with 10 cm long blue fringe, sewn on lower end and selvedges.
Design and ornaments: pentagonal central field with diagonal lattice design formed by elongated leaf-like toothed figures; seated birds inscribed in compartments; central field framed by three borders with main one decorated with the *ovadan* meander on a white ground (design changes at top) and minor ones carrying the *sarkhalka* design.
Published: Pinner, Franses 1980, pl. VII.
Analogies: see No. 44.

44
Tekke asmalyk

151×88 cm

18th century
Museum of Ethnography, Leningrad.
No. 26-52/1

Warp: ivory wool, Z2S.
Weft: two shoots, camel hair, Z2.
Pile: wool, lightly twisted, Z2S.
Knot: asymmetrical, open on right (ASII).
Knot density: 2,236 knots per dm^2 (1:1.5), pile height 3 mm.
Dyes: natural.
Colours (six): red, orange-red, brown, dark blue, sky-blue, white.
Finish: selvedges—red wool, wrapped round two warps; upper end—white plain weave, folded over on back and sewn down; plaited band, attached to corners; lower end—red plain weave, folded over on back and sewn down; broad patterned tape, sewn on lower end and selvedges; 10 cm long blue woollen fringe, attached to outer edge.
Design and ornaments: pentagonal central field with diagonal lattice design formed by elongated leaf-like toothed figures; each compartment carries representations of a running bird (bustard?) and a small two-headed animal; central field framed by three borders, of which main one is decorated with the *ovadan* meander which changes into a diamond-type pattern on top, while two minor borders carry the *giyak* design; *elem* panels undecorated (extremely narrow on top).
Published: Pinner, Franses 1980, pl. VI; Felkerzam 1914, pp. 34–35.
Analogies: Pinner, Franses 1980, ill. 216–230, pl. 1, 7/9; Moshkova 1970, fig. 61.

43

44

45
Tekke asmalyk

128×82 cm

19th century
The Hermitage, Leningrad. No. VT-716

Warp: ivory wool, mixed with dark brown, Z2S.
Weft: very fine, two shoots, light brown wool, Z2S.
Pile: wool, Z2S.
Knot: asymmetrical, open on right (ASII).
Knot density: 3,080 knots per dm^2 (1:1.6), pile height 3.5 mm.
Dyes: natural.
Colours (six): cherry-red, orange-red, brown, mid-blue, blue-green, white.
Finish: selvedges—red wool, wrapped round two warps; upper end—0.5 cm red plain weave, folded over and sewn down on front; 1.5 cm white plain weave, folded over on back and sewn down; lower end—1 cm white plain weave, folded over on front; 4 cm wide woven band with dark blue fringe sewn on selvedges and lower end.

Design and ornaments: pentagonal central field with diagonal lattice design formed by elongated leaf-like toothed figures; large flowers and minute zoomorphic figures inscribed in compartments; central field framed by three borders with main one decorated with the *ovadan* meander on a white ground and two minor borders decorated with the *sarkhalka* motif; at top design changes into geometrical diamonds.

First publication.
Analogies: Felkerzam 1914, pp. 90–91; Pinner, Franses 1980, pl. X, ill. 231–236.

45

46
Tekke asmalyk

132×82 cm

18th or first half 19th century
Museum of Oriental Art, Moscow.
No. 2645 III

Warp: white wool, Z2S.
Weft: two shoots, light brown wool, lightly twisted, Z2S.
Pile: wool, Z2S.
Knot: asymmetrical, open on right (ASII).
Knot density: 3,528 knots per dm² (1:2), pile height 3 mm.
Dyes: natural.
Colours (eight): red, terracotta-red, orange-red, brown, mid-blue, sky-blue, blue-green, white.
Finish: selvedges—two pairs of warps, overcast with orange and red wool; upper end—white plain weave, folded over on back; 12 cm wide brown plaited band, sewn on; lower end—red plain weave (0.5 cm) and white plain weave (1.5 cm), remainder missing.
Design and ornaments: pentagonal central field with diagonal lattice design formed by elongated leaf-like toothed figures; representations of seated birds inscribed in compartments; central field framed below and along sides by three borders and at top by one border with diamond-type design; main border decorated with the *ovadan* meander on a white ground and two minor borders with the *sarkhalka* design.

Published: Beresneva 1976, pl. 14.
Analogies: see No. 44.

46

47

47
Tekke horse trappings

128×86 cm

Late 19th century
Museum of Ethnography, Leningrad.
No. 87-15

Warp: white wool, Z2S.
Weft: one shoot, white wool, mixed with grey, Z1S.
Pile: wool, Z2S.
Knot: asymmetrical, open on right (ASII).
Knot density: 3,948 knots per dm^2 (1:2.2), pile height 5 mm.
Dyes: natural and synthetic.
Colours (eight): crimson, bright red, orange, yellow, brown, mid-blue, blue-green, white.
Finish: selvedges—dark blue wool, wrapped round two pairs of warps; silk plaited band with 10 cm long fringe, sewn on sides and top; ends—red and white plain weave, folded over on back and sewn down; plaited silk band, stitched onto front.
Design and ornaments: rectangular central field with straight *aina gochak* lattice design; at top pentagon formed by a stripe with the *gochak* motif and filled with the *kelle* design; entire composition framed by three borders; main one carries *khamtoz* diamonds framed by zigzags; outer minor border decorated with the *giyak* design and inner one, as well as stripe separating compartments, with the *khamtoz* motif; at bottom narrow strip with star-shaped design on a white ground.

First publication.
No near analogies identified.

48 →
Tekke chuval

135×78 cm

19th century
Museum of Oriental Art, Moscow.
No. 1267 III

Warp: white wool, Z2S.
Weft: two shoots, brown wool, lightly twisted, Z2S.
Pile: wool, Z2S, Z3S.
Knot: asymmetrical, open on right (ASII), eleven end rows with symmetrical knots.
Knot density: 2,508 knots per dm^2 (1:1.7), pile height 5 mm.
Dyes: natural.
Colours (seven): two shades of bright red, orange, dark brown, dark blue, light blue, white.
Finish: selvedges—two pairs of warps, overcast with brown wool; upper end—0.5 cm bluish-green plain weave, folded over and sewn down on front; 0.5 cm sky-blue plain weave followed by 2.5 cm ivory plain weave, folded over and sewn on back; lower end—4 cm light brown plain weave, folded over on back and sewn down.
Design and ornaments: rectangular central field with 3 by 4 rows of *chuval göls* (old version) and secondary *chemche* designs; central field framed by three borders with four intermediate *giyak* stripes; main border decorated with a variation of the *gochak* (?) design and minor ones with a variation of the *dogajik* motif; broad lower *elem* panel has three *kelle* figures of unusual design; side and top *elem* panels undecorated; narrow stripe with the *giyak* motif on top.

First publication.
Analogies: Mackie, Thompson 1980, pl. 30.

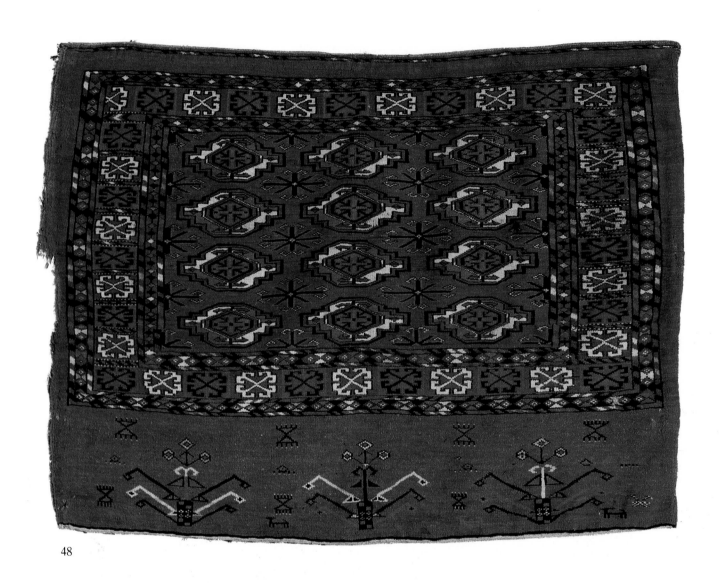

48

49

Tekke chuval

120×85 cm

Late 18th or early 19th century
Museum of Ethnography, Leningrad.
No. 2268-"T"

Warp: white wool, finely spun, Z2S.
Weft: two shoots, very fine, brown wool, Z2S.
Pile: wool, Z2S.
Knot: asymmetrical, open on right (ASII), pile turned upwards.
Knot density: 3,276 knots per dm^2 (1:1.8), pile height 2 mm.
Dyes: natural.
Colours (eight): violet-brown, orange-red, yellow, light brown, mid-blue, green, greenish-blue, ivory.
Finish: selvedges missing; upper end—1 cm bluish-green and red plain weave, folded over and sewn down on front; 3 cm white plain weave, folded over and sewn on back; lower end—blue and red plain weave, remainder cut.
Design and ornaments: rectangular central field with 5 by 5 rows of *chuval göls* (old version) and secondary *chemche* designs; central field framed by three borders with main one decorated with the *aina* design and minor ones with the *giyak* motif; broad lower *elem* panel has 4 by 8 rows of small geometrical figures with protective symbolism (design unidentified); upper *elem* panel has small *dogajik* figures alternating with crosslike figures; top border carries geometrical design.

First publication.
No near analogies identified.

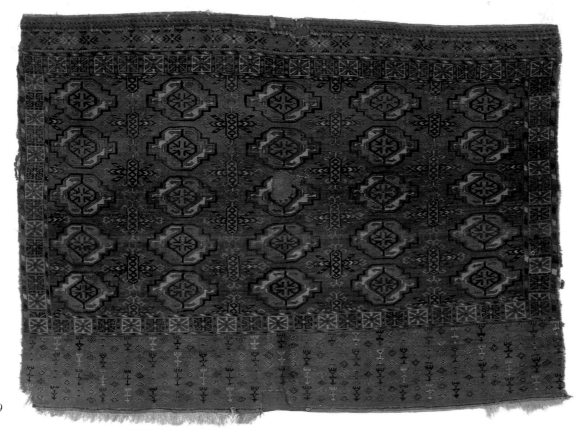

49

50
Tekke chuval

116×84 cm

Early 19th century
Museum of Ethnography, Leningrad.
No. 2019-3

Warp: ivory wool, Z2S.
Weft: two shoots, fine, brown wool, Z2S.
Pile: wool, Z2S.
Knot: asymmetrical, open on right (ASII).
Knot density: 2,640 knots per dm^2 (1:1.4), pile height 2 mm
Dyes: natural.
Colours (seven): violet-red, crimson, orange, brown, dark blue, bluish-green, white.
Finish: selvedges missing; upper end—green plain weave, folded over on back and sewn down; lower end—ivory plain weave with green stripe, remainder missing.
Design and ornaments: rectangular central field with 5 by 4 rows of *chuval göls* (old version) and secondary *chemche* designs; central field framed by three borders with main one having unidentified geometrical design and minor ones having the *giyak* motif; broad lower *elem* panel carries eight upright figures resembling stalks and flowers; upper narrow *elem* panel undecorated; upper border has the *giyak* and *alaja* motifs.

First publication.
Analogies: Mackie, Thompson 1980, fig. 65 (main border, *elem* panel).

51
Tekke torba

100×52 cm

Not later than mid-19th century
Museum of Ethnography, Leningrad.
No. 4712-5

Warp: ivory wool, Z2S.
Weft: two shoots, brown wool, lightly twisted and lightly spun, Z2S.
Pile: wool, Z2S.
Knot: asymmetrical, open on right (ASII).
Knot density: 2,365 knots per dm^2 (1:1.6), pile height 4.5 mm.
Dyes: natural.
Colours (six): light terracotta-red, orange, dark brown, dark blue, sky-blue, ivory.
Finish: selvedges—two warps, wrapped with wool coloured as ground; at bottom 16 cm of edge, oversewn with orange and blue wool; upper end—2 cm brown plain weave, folded over on front and sewn down; 2 cm ivory plain weave, folded over on back and sewn down; lower end cut.
Design and ornaments: rectangular central field with 4.5 by 3 rows of *dyrnak göls* and secondary diamond-shaped designs; central field framed by three borders with main one decorated with the *tekbent* design and two minor ones with the *giyak* motif; broad *elem* panels, undecorated; top stripe carries the *giyak* motif.

First publication.
Analogies: Mackie, Thompson 1980, pl. 38; Thacher 1977, pl. 23 (basic element of central field).

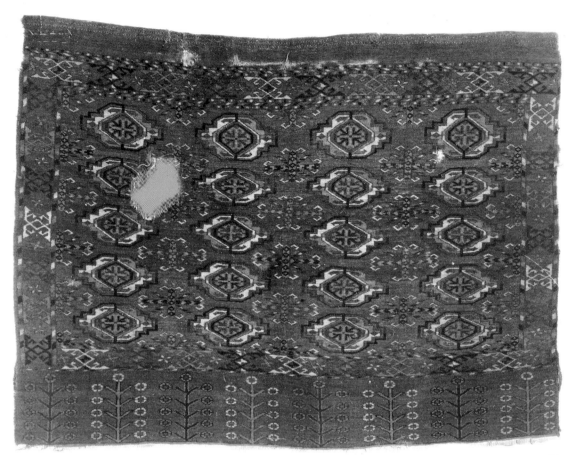

50

51

52
Tekke chuval

113×66 cm

19th century
The Russian Museum, Leningrad.
No. KOB-188

Warp: ivory wool, Z2S.
Weft: one shoot, very fine, ivory wool, Z2S.
Pile: wool and silk, Z2S.
Knot: asymmetrical, open on right (ASII), *elem* panel woven very unevenly.
Knot density: 5,500 knots per dm² (1:2.2), pile height 3 mm.
Dyes: natural.
Colours (eight): red, red-orange, crimson (silk), brown, dark blue, green-blue, green, sky-blue (last two only in *elem* panel).
Finish: selvedges—two pairs of warps, oversewn with red wool; upper end—blue plain weave, folded over and sewn down on front; ivory plain weave, folded over and sewn on back; lower end missing.
Design and ornaments: rectangular central field with 5 by 6 rows of small *chuval göls* and secondary *chemche* designs; central field framed by three borders with four intermediate *giyak* stripes: main border decorated with the *kojanak* design and minor ones with the *chetanak* motif; lower *elem* panel has sixteen rows of *kelle* figures in two variations, one akin to the Chodor version.

First publication.
Analogies: Pinner, Franses 1980, pl. 243; Thacher 1977, pl. 12.

52

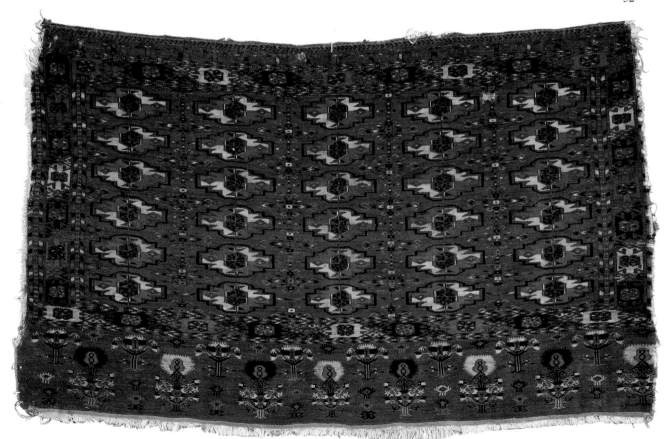

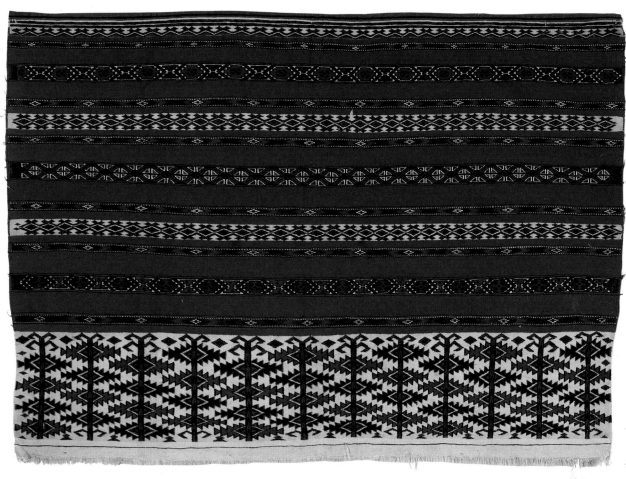

53

53

Tekke ak chuval

109×77 cm

Second half 19th century
Museum of Ethnography, Leningrad.
No. 26-81

Warp: ivory wool, Z2S.
Weft: one shoot, ivory wool for white ground, brown wool for red ground and white cotton for *elem* panel, Z2S.
Pile: wool and cotton, Z2S.
Knot: asymmetrical, open on right (ASII), strips of pile fabric alternate with strips of plain weave.
Knot density: 5,096 knots per dm^2 (1:1.9), pile height 1 mm.
Dyes: natural.
Colours (eight): light terracotta-red, magenta red, bright-red, crimson, brown, blue, green, white (cotton).
Finish: selvedges—two pairs of warps, overcast with red wool and white cotton (in *elem* panel); upper end—red and white plain weave, folded over on back and sewn down; lower end—white plain weave, cut.

Design and ornaments: banded pattern of decorated pile and undecorated red plain weave; three patterns used on five decorated bands; central band carries the *gara nagysh* pattern; two bands have unidentified geometrical diamond design; two outer bands contain the *gochak* design; narrow stripes between broader bands carry the *khamtoz* motif; broad bottom *elem* panel decorated with the *kelle* motif on a white ground.

First publication.
Analogies: McMullan, Reichert 1970, pl. 68.

54

Tekke torba

110×36 cm

19th century
Museum of Ethnography, Leningrad.
No. 26-15

Warp: white wool, fine, Z2S.
Weft: two shoots, brown wool, lightly spun and twisted, Z2S.
Pile: wool and cotton, Z2.
Knot: asymmetrical, open on right (ASII).
Knot density: 8,100 knots per dm^2 (1:2.8), pile height 2.5 mm.
Dyes: natural.
Colours (nine): light-red, orange-red, light crimson, yellow, dark brown, dark blue, sky-blue, green-blue, white (cotton).
Finish: selvedges—two pairs of warps, oversewn with red wool; 1.8 cm wide red and blue plaited band, ending in tassel at bottom; long strings at top, sewn on sides; back and face sewn together; upper end—0.3 cm sky-blue plain weave and 1.2 cm red plain weave, folded over on back and sewn down;

lower end—0.3 cm green plain weave followed by white plain weave, folded over on back to form back of bag; fringe of pile colours knotted on four warps.
Design and ornaments: rectangular central field with 3 by 3 rows of *chuval göls* enclosing complex design and secondary *chemche* designs; central field framed by three borders; main one decorated with the *kojanak* motif and minor ones with the *giyak* design; *elem* panels, undecorated; top stripe has the *giyak* motif.

First publication.
Analogies: Azadi 1975, pl. 24.

54

55

Tekke torba

107×42 cm

Not later than mid-19th century
Museum of Ethnography, Leningrad.
No. 26-78

Warp: ivory wool, Z2S.
Weft: one shoot, grey wool, mixed with brown, Z2S.
Pile: wool, Z2; silk, Z2; cotton, lightly spun and twisted, Z2S.
Knot: asymmetrical, open on right (ASII), two side rows with symmetrical knots.
Knot density: 5,300 knots per dm² (1:2.1), pile height 3 mm.
Dyes: natural.
Colours (eleven): bright red, light red, crimson (silk), orange, yellow, brown, dark blue, bluish-green, green, ivory, white (cotton).
Finish: selvedges—two pairs of warps, oversewn with red wool; upper end—plain weave with one white weft, 0.5 cm red plain weave, 2 cm white plain weave, folded over on back and sewn down; lower end—light brown plain weave forms back of torba; 33 cm long multi-coloured fringe, knotted on four warps.

Design and ornaments: rectangular central field with straight lattice design formed by strips with the *khamtoz* motif, with *sekme gül* designs in compartments; central field framed by three borders and additional vertical band with the *tekbent* design; main border decorated with the *kojanak* design and minor ones with the *giyak* motif which changes into the *ala govurdak* design at the top.

First publication.
Analogies: *Hali*, 1978, vol. 1, No. 1, p. 41; Thacher 1977, table 15 (central field).

55

56
Tekke mafrach

76×30 cm

19th century
The Russian Museum, Leningrad.
No. KOB-181

Warp: ivory wool, Z2S.
Weft: two shoots, very fine, light brown wool, Z2S.
Pile: wool, silk, cotton, lightly spun, Z2S.
Knot: asymmetrical, open on right (ASII).
Knot density: 4,284 knots per dm^2 (1:2.4), pile height 2.5 mm.
Dyes: natural.
Colours (eight): cherry-red, crimson (silk), orange, yellow, brown, mid-blue, green, white (wool and cotton).
Finish: selvedges—bottom 5 cm wrapped with crimson and green silk; 1.5 cm wide red and green plaited band, sewn on; upper end—2 cm dark blue plain weave, folded over on back and sewn down; 2 cm ivory plain weave, folded over on back and sewn down; lower end—0.5 cm red plain weave followed by trimmed band on ivory fabric; multi-coloured fringe, knotted on four warps.
Design and ornaments: rectangular central field with straight 4 by 3 lattice design with *aina gochak* figures in compartments; central field framed by three borders with main one decorated with *khamtoz*-type motifs, framed by zigzags, and minor ones decorated with the *khamtoz* design; *elem* panels, undecorated; top narrow stripe carries geometrical design.

First publication.
Analogies: Jones, Boucher 1973, No. 7; Pinner, Franses 1980, pl. 152; Roberts 1981, pl. 37 (design of central field).

57
Tekke mafrach

84×29 cm

First half 19th century
The Russian Museum, Leningrad.
No. KOB-210

Warp: ivory wool, Z2S.
Weft: one shoot, white wool with some brown, Z2.
Pile: wool and cotton, Z2S.
Knot: asymmetrical, open on right (ASII), pile turned upwards.
Knot density: 4,992 knots per dm^2 (1:2.2), pile height 2 mm.
Dyes: natural.
Colours (six): red, orange, brown, dark blue, bluish-green, white (cotton).
Finish: selvedges—wrapped with red wool later; upper end—blue plain weave, folded over on front and sewn down; ivory plain weave, folded over on back and sewn down; lower end missing.
Design and ornaments: rectangular central field with straight 6 by 4 lattice design with octagonals enclosing crosslike motif in compartments formed by stripes, carrying *alaja* speckles; central field framed by three borders with main one decorated with straight lattice designs enclosing crosslike motifs and minor ones with the *giyak* motif; *elem* panels, undecorated; top stripe contains the *giyak* motif.

First publication.
Analogies: "Small is Beautiful. The Yomut Mafrash", *Hali*, 1981, vol. 4, No. 1, p. 11, pl. 7.

56

57

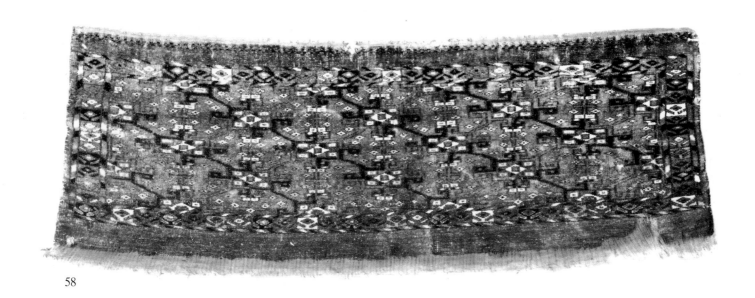

58

59

58
Tekke mafrach

60×28 cm

Not later than early 19th century
The Russian Museum, Leningrad.
No. KOB-211

Warp: ivory wool, fine, Z2S.
Weft: one shoot, ivory wool, mixed with brown, Z2S.
Pile: wool, Z2S; silk, Z2S, Z3S.
Knot: asymmetrical, open on right (ASII), pile turned upwards.
Knot density: 3,956 knots per dm² (1:1.8), pile height 3 mm.
Dyes: natural.
Colours (ten): red-brown, crimson-red, crimson (silk), orange, yellow, violet-brown, brown, mid-blue, green, ivory.
Finish: selvedges—cut and later wrapped; upper end—red plain weave, folded over on front and sewn down; ivory plain weave, folded over on back and sewn down; lower end missing.
Design and ornaments: rectangular central field with diagonal lattice design formed by junction of corners of horned *göl*-type figures of dark and light tones in checkerboard arrangement; central field framed by three borders with main one having straight lattice design with unidentified trefoil-type motifs inscribed in each compartment, and two minor ones decorated with the *giyak* design; *elem* panels, undecorated; top stripe has two rows of *alaja* motifs.

First publication.
No analogies identified.

59
Tekke mafrach

76×34 cm

19th century
The Russian Museum, Leningrad.
No. KOB-241

Warp: ivory wool, Z2S.
Weft: two shoots, grey wool, mixed with white and brown, Z1.
Pile: wool, Z2S.
Knot: asymmetrical, open on right (ASI).
Knot density: 2,520 knots per dm² (1:2), pile height 4.5 mm.
Dyes: natural.
Colours (eight): dark red, orange, yellow, brown, dark blue, sky-blue, blue-green, white.
Finish: selvedges—blue wool, wrapped round two warps; upper end—red plain weave, folded over on front and sewn down; ivory plain weave, folded over on back and sewn down; lower end—warps end in tassels; sky-blue and orange woollen fringe, attached.
Design and ornaments: rectangular central field with 14 by 6 rows of small *dogajik* figures coloured in dark and light tones; framed by five borders with main one having unidentified flower-like design; narrow borders decorated with the *giyak* and *chetanak* designs.

First publication.
Analogies: Pinner, Franses 1980, pl. 402 (central field).

60
Tekke mafrach

76×37 cm

19th century
The Russian Museum, Leningrad.
No. KOB-161

Warp: ivory wool, Z2S.
Weft: two shoots, light brown wool, Z2.
Pile: wool and silk, Z2S.
Knot: asymmetrical open on right (ASII).
Knot density: 3,496 knots per dm^2 (1:1.7), pile height 2 mm.
Dyes: natural.
Colours (eight): red, orange, yellow, pink (silk), brown, mid-blue, green, ivory.
Finish: selvedges—several warp cables, oversewn with red wool; face and back sewn together with blue and red tasselled plaited band sewn on seam; upper end—red plain weave, folded over on front and sewn down; ivory plain weave, folded over on back and sewn down; lower end—ivory plain weave continues to form back of bag; remains of woollen fringe of pile colours, knotted on four warps.
Design and ornaments: rectangular central field, with three vertical panels decorated with large stylized flowers and numerous small floral motifs on a white ground; central field framed by two broad borders with three intermediate stripes; inner border has straight lattice design with unidentified trefoil-type motif which is also on stripes separating central field panels; outer border decorated with the *ak gyra* design and separates intermediate stripes with the *giyak* motif, a variation of which is also carried by top stripe.

First publication.
Analogies: Pinner, Franses 1980, figs. 405, 406; "Small is Beautiful. The Yomut Mafrash", *Hali*, 1981, vol. 4, No. 1, pl. 21; Thacher 1977, pls. 26, 27 (central field and several borders).

61
Tekke mafrach

78×34 cm

19th century
The Russian Museum, Leningrad.
No. KOB-208

Warp: ivory wool, lightly twisted, Z2S.
Weft: two shoots, one of pink-dyed wool, the other of white wool with some brown, lightly twisted, Z2S.
Pile: wool, Z2S.
Knot: asymmetrical, open on right (ASI).
Knot density: 4,208 knots per dm^2 (1:1.8), pile height 3 mm.
Dyes: natural.
Colours (eight): cherry-red, orange, yellow, brown, dark blue, sky-blue, green-blue, white.
Finish: selvedges—red wool, wrapped round two pairs of warps; upper end—blue plain weave on face; ivory plain weave on back; strings of blue-red plaited band with tassels sewn onto corners; lower end cut; remains of blue and red fringe, knotted on four warps; multi-coloured 17 cm long woollen fringe, attached later.
Design and ornaments: rectangular central field divided into seven vertical bands with alternating motifs, some having small diagonally coloured lattice, others vertical nests of figures with horn-shaped designs; central field framed by three borders with unidentified geometrical spear-shaped design on main border and the *saldat* design on minor ones; broad *elem* panels decorated with the *khamtoz* design; top stripe carries variations of the *giyak* motif.

First publication.
Analogies: Gombos 1975, pl. 56 (design of central field).

60

61

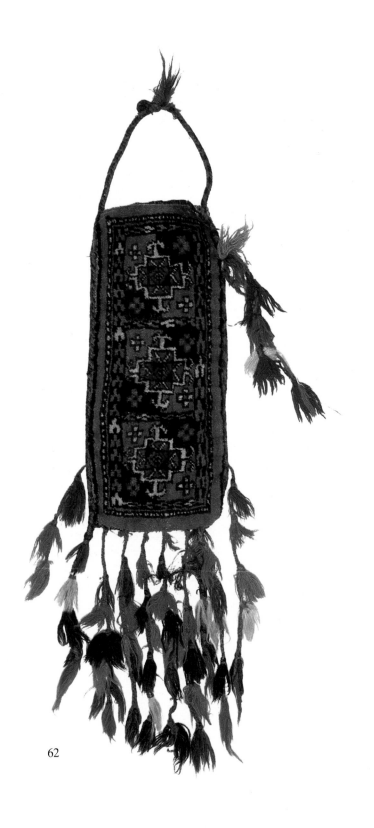

62

62
Tekke aina khalta

19×42 cm

Late 19th century
The Russian Museum, Leningrad.
No. KOB-196

Warp: ivory wool, Z2S.
Weft: two shoots, light brown wool, Z2S.
Pile: wool, Z2S.
Knot: symmetrical (SYI).
Knot density: 2,240 knots per dm^2 (1:1.3), pile height 8 mm.
Dyes: natural and synthetic.
Colours (seven): orange-red, bright red, orange, brown, sky-blue, green, white.
Finish: selvedges—two pairs of warps overcast with blue wool; ends—ivory plain weave; top and selvedges oversewn with blue and red wool, ending in a loop; selvedges and lower end embellished with multi-tiered, multi-coloured tassels.
Design and ornaments: rectangular central field divided vertically into three compartments, each enclosing the *aina gochak* motif; framed by borders with the *saldat* and *alaja* motifs; *elem* panels, undecorated.

First publication.
No analogies identified.

63

63
Tekke mafrach

74×25 cm

> 18th century
> Museum of Oriental Art, Moscow.
> No. 2645-III

Warp: camel hair, Z2S.
Weft: two shoots, light brown wool, Z1.
Pile: wool, Z2S.
Knot: asymmetrical open on right (ASII), pile turned upwards.
Knot density: 6,120 knots per dm² (1:2.4), pile height 2.5–3 mm.
Dyes: natural.
Colours (seven): two shades of red, two shades of brown, dark blue, blue-green, ivory.
Finish: selvedges—dark blue wool, wrapped round two warps; blue and red braided cord, sewn on at side; blue, green and red plaited band with strings attached to upper corners; upper end—3 cm red plain weave, folded over on front and sewn down; 1.4 cm white plain weave, folded over on back and sewn down; lower end—0.5 cm red plain weave and 37 cm long warp ends, wrapped (in groups of four) with multi-coloured wool of pile colours.
Design and ornaments: rectangular central field with diagonal *kelle* figures in light and dark tones in checkerboard arrangement; central field framed by two broad borders with two intermediate stripes; inner border decorated with a variation of the *gochak* motif, outer one with row of small zoomorphic figures; intermediate stripes with the *giyak* motif; top stripe has two rows of *alaja* motifs.

Published: Beresneva 1976, pl. 19.
No analogies identified.

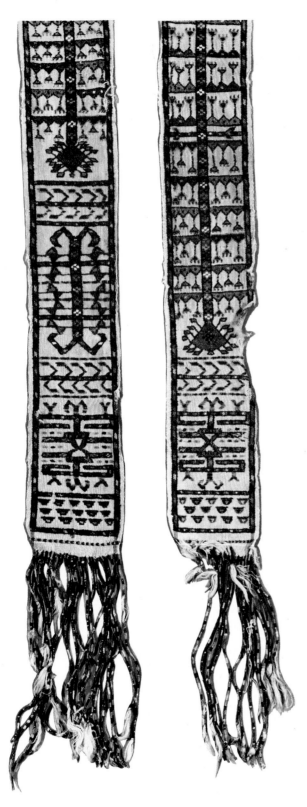

64

64
Tekke iolam (fragment)

282×16 cm

First half 19th century
The Russian Museum, Leningrad,
No. KOB-171

Warp: ivory wool, very fine, Z2S.
Weft: white cotton, very fine, Z2S.
Pile: wool and cotton, Z2S; silk, Z3.
Knot: symmetrical, single level.
Knot density: 3,332 knots per dm² (1:1.3), pile height 3 mm (frayed).
Dyes: natural.
Colours (nine): brown-red, orange-red, crimson (silk), yellow, brown, mid-blue, sky-blue, green, white (cotton and very little wool).
Finish: selvedges—no additions; ends—wool of pile colours, wrapped round warps.
Design and ornaments: all elements of stylized floral and horn-shaped decoration organized symmetrically with respect to central axial band carrying the *khamtoz* motif; some motifs separated by transverse stripes decorated with geometrical design.

First publication.
No near analogies identified.

65
Tekke iolam

1,400×30 cm

Second half 19th century
Museum of Ethnography, Leningrad.
No. 115-8

Warp: ivory wool, very fine, Z2S.
Weft: ivory wool, very fine, Z2S.
Pile: wool and silk, Z2S.
Knot: symmetrical, single level.
Knot density: 4,608 knots per dm² (1:1.1), pile height 2 mm.
Dyes: natural.
Colours (ten): red, orange, pink (silk), bright red, yellow, dark blue, blue-green, light green (silk), mid-green (silk), olive-green (silk).
Finish: selvedges—red wool wrapped round two warps; ends—plain weave with brocaded design, finished with red and blue cord braided on four warps; warps end in 60 cm long braided cords.
Design and ornaments: all elements of stylized floral geometrical and horn-shaped decoration organized symmetrically with respect to the central axial band; some motifs divided by transverse bands with geometrical design.

First publication.
No analogies identified.

65

66
Yomud khali (fragment)

160 cm wide

Not later than early 19th century
Museum of Ethnography, Leningrad.
No. 1697-1

Warp: white wool, Z2S.
Weft: two shoots, fine, light brown wool, Z2S.
Pile: wool, Z2S.
Knot: symmetrical (SYI)
Knot density: 1,800 knots per dm² (1:2), pile height 4 mm.
Dyes: natural.
Colours (eight): violet-brown, bright red, yellow, dark brown, mid-blue, sky-blue, green, white.
Finish: selvedges—violet-brown wool wrapped round one pair of warps; ends missing.
Design and ornaments: rectangular central field with offset rows of *göls* with toothed leaves; central field framed by three borders with four intermediate stripes decorated with the *alaja* design; main border decorated with the *syrga* motif, two minor borders with variation of the *khamtoz* design; *elem* panels decorated with offset rows of figures resembling plants with long and curved toothed leaves.

Publication: Felkerzam 1914, pp. 82–83.
Analogies: Mackie, Thompson 1980, pl. 64 (central field, borders); Azadi 1975, pl. 11 (basic element of central field).

66

67
Yomud khali

340×190 cm

19th century
Museum of Ethnography, Leningrad.
No. 4710-3

Warp: white wool, Z2S.
Weft: two shoots, light brown wool, Z2S.
Pile: wool, Z2S.
Knot: symmetrical (SYI).
Knot density: 1,860 knots per dm² (1:2), pile height 4 mm.
Dyes: natural.
Colours (seven): violet-brown, bright red, dark yellow, dark brown, dark blue, green, white.
Finish: selvedges—dark blue wool, wrapped round four warps; ends—7 cm violet-brown and white plain weave with embroidered decorative stripe; warps end in fringe; remains of strings of braided warps, at corners.
Design and ornaments: rectangular central field with 3 by 10 rows of *dyrnak göls* and secondary ornaments with another variation of same design; central field framed by three borders with four intermediate stripes carrying the *giyak* motif; main border has vertical meander with representations of stylized two-headed animals and horizontally placed *dogajik* design; minor inner border contains unidentified diagonal lattice design; minor outer border carries the *gochak* design; broad *elem* panels on ends decorated with the *erre* design.

First publication.
Analogies: Gombos 1975, pl. 10 (central field, broad transverse border).

68 →
Yomud khali

340×190 cm

19th century
Museum of Ethnography, Leningrad.
No. 4710-2

Warp: white wool, Z2S.
Weft: two shoots, light brown wool, Z2S.
Pile: wool, Z2S.
Knot: symmetrical (SYI).
Knot density: 1,860 knots per dm² (1:2), pile height 4 mm.
Dyes: natural.
Colours (seven): violet-brown, bright red, dark yellow, dark brown, dark blue, green, white.
Finish: selvedges—dark blue wool, wrapped round four warps; ends—7 cm violet-brown and white plain weave with embroidered decorative stripe; warps end in fringe; strings of braided warps attached to upper corners.
Design and ornaments: rectangular central field with 3 by 12 rows of *dyrnak göls* and secondary offset rows of *dyrnak göls*; central field framed by four borders, with main one carrying a variation of the *dogajik* motif and minor ones the *khamtoz* design; outer narrow border decorated with the *giyak* motif; *elem* panels on ends carry the *kelle* design.

First publication.
No near analogies identified.

69

← 69
Yomud khali

306×165 cm

Last third 19th century
Museum of Ethnography, Leningrad.
No. 4501-1

Warp: grey wool, mixed with white, Z2S.
Weft: two shoots, very fine, light brown wool, Z2S.
Pile: wool, Z2S.
Knot: symmetrical (SYI).
Knot density: 2,506 knots per dm^2 (1:1.6), pile height 5 mm.
Dyes: natural and synthetic.
Colours (five): violet-brown, bright red, dark brown, dark blue, white.
Finish: selvedges—no additional work, thick blue selvedge, stitched along entire length and wrapped together with outer warp row with blue wool; ends missing.
Design and ornaments: rectangular central field with 4 by 13 rows of *chuval göls* and secondary *chemche* designs; central field framed by three borders with main one decorated with meander carrying *dyrnak göl*-type figures, vertical narrow borders have the *gochak* motif and horizontal narrow borders the *khamtoz* motif; *elem* panels on ends decorated with six large floral motifs.

First publication.
No near analogies identified.

70
Yomud khali

285×187 cm

Second half 19th century
The Russian Museum, Leningrad.
No. KOB-175

Warp: ivory wool, Z2S.
Weft: two shoots, brown wool, Z2S.
Pile: wool, Z2S.
Knot: symmetrical (SYI).
Knot density: 1,872 knots per dm^2 (1:1.5), pile height 6 mm.
Dyes: natural.
Colours (seven): violet-brown, bright red, orange, brown, mid-blue, blue-green, ivory.
Finish: selvedges—three pairs of warps, overcast with blue wool; ends—red plain weave, followed by white plain weave with red stripe; blue and red braided cord woven in; warps end in 27 cm long fringe.
Design and ornaments: rectangular central field with offset rows of *kapsa göls*; central field framed by three borders with main one decorated with a variation of the *ovadan* motif and minor ones with the *sary ichyan* design; side *elem* panels undecorated; end *elem* panels with the *erre* design.

First publication.
Analogies: Azadi 1975, pl. 14; Roberts 1981, pl. 57; Thacher 1977, pl. 20 (some borders, basic element of central field).

70

71

71
Yomud ensi

126×169 cm

Second half 19th century
Museum of Ethnography, Leningrad.
No. 5117-1

Warp: white wool, Z2S.
Weft: two shoots, red-dyed wool, Z2.
Pile: wool, Z2S.
Knot: symmetrical (SYI).
Knot density: 2,040 knots per dm^2 (1:1.8), pile height 3 mm.
Dyes: natural and synthetic (?).
Colours (seven): violet-brown, bright red, mid-brown, dark brown with olive-green tint, dark blue, green, ivory.
Finish: selvedges—cut and later wrapped; upper end—1 cm violet-brown plain weave on face; blue and red braided cord woven in; 2 cm similar fabric, folded over on back and sewn down; lower end missing.
Design and ornaments: rectangular central field divided into four panels by two bands in cross-shape; each panel filled with rows of small *gush* figures; transverse band of three rows with four secondary *giyak* motifs; broad central row carries a variation of the *gochak* design and narrow rows decorated with the *khamtoz* motif; vertical band also of three rows; main one carries a variation of the *govacha gül* design and narrow side rows the *saldat* design; row of *bovrek* figures flanks both sides of the vertical band; entire composition framed on three sides by arch formed by meander with the *ovadan* motif and secondary *gozenek* figures and by a continuous border around the central field with the *govacha gül* design; at the lower end is a panel with small *kelle* figures; outer framing border forms an arch with the *ovadan* meander design similar to the central field border; bottom *elem* panel with seven large *kelle* figures framed by border with the *uriuk gül* design.

First publication.
No near analogies identified.

72 →
Yomud ensi

157×126 cm

Second half 19th century
The Russian Museum, Leningrad.
No. KOB-168

Warp: ivory wool, S2Z.
Weft: two shoots, brown wool, Z2S.
Pile: wool, Z2S.
Knot: symmetrical (SYI).
Knot density: 1,994 knots per dm^2 (1:2), pile height 3 mm (frayed).
Dyes: natural.
Colours (eight): violet-brown, red, orange, dark brown, dark blue, blue-green, mid-green, ivory.
Finish: selvedges—dark blue wool, wrapped round one and two pairs of warps; upper end—1 cm violet-brown plain weave, remainder missing; lower end—4 cm ivory plain weave, violet-brown near pile; blue and red braided cord, woven in below.
Design and ornaments: entire surface with exception of *elem* panel decorated with variations of the *dogajik* design; rectangular central field divided by two bands in cross-shape; one vertical band flanked by rows of *bovrek* motifs; three horizontal bands with intermediate *gozenek* stripes; central field framed by three borders; bottom *elem* panel with large floral-type figures above and the *erre* design below.

First publication.
No near analogies identified.

72

73
Yomud ensi

176×132 cm

Second half 19th century
The Russian Museum, Leningrad.
No. KOB-169

Warp: white wool, mixed with grey, Z2S.
Weft: two shoots, one strand dark brown wool, Z2S, the other white cotton, Z2S.
Pile: wool, Z2S, Z3S, Z4S.
Knot: symmetrical (SYI).
Knot density: 1,560 knots per dm^2 (1:1.7), pile height 2 mm (frayed).
Dyes: natural.
Colours (seven): light brown with violet tinge, red, orange, dark brown, dark blue, bluish-green, ivory.
Finish: selvedges—two pairs of warps, overcast with red and bluish-green wool; ends—white (cotton) plain weave; multi-coloured braided cord, woven in; warps end in fringe.
Design and ornaments: rectangular central field divided into four panels by two bands in cross-shape each filled with checkerboard arrangement of rows of diamond-shaped figures; transverse and longitudinal bands both decorated with a variation of the *tekbent* motif; vertical side border nearest field carries the *giyak* design, horizontal border carries a chain of diamonds; next to vertical border on the side of the panels is a row of *bovrek* figures; the entire composition framed by three borders with same decoration as that of transverse band in central field; *elem* panel has two offset rows of large *kelle* figures, eight at top and nine at bottom on an olive-brown ground.

First publication.
No near analogies identified.

73

74
Yomud asmalyk

137×90 cm

Not later than first half 19th century
The Russian Museum, Leningrad.
No. KOB-207

Warp: white wool, mixed with grey and brown, Z2S.
Weft: two shoots, very fine, brown wool, Z2S.
Pile: wool, Z2S.
Knot: symmetrical (SYI).
Knot density: 3,360 knots per dm² (1:2.1), pile height 4 mm.
Dyes: natural.
Colours (seven): bright red, violet-brown, dark brown, mid-blue, light blue, green, ivory.
Finish: selvedges—no additional work; ends—1.5 cm red plain weave, folded over on back and sewn down; sides and bottom finished with brocaded band; 16 cm long dark blue fringe, attached; multi-coloured plaited strings, sewn onto upper corners.
Design and ornaments: octagonal central field with five vertical figures reminiscent of plants; main border on three sides with the *gochak* design; flanked by minor borders with the *saldat* motif, at top decoration changes into diagonal lattice design of small diamonds; narrow undecorated side *elem* panel; broad bottom *elem* panel carries band of small *gochak* designs in checkerboard arrangement.

First publication.
Analogies: Mackie, Thompson 1980, pl. 77.

74

75

Yomud asmalyk

134×83 cm

19th century
The Russian Museum, Leningrad.
No. KOB-167

Warp: ivory wool, Z2S.
Weft: two shoots, ivory wool, Z2S.
Pile: wool, Z2S.
Knot: symmetrical (SYI).
Knot density: 2,520 knots per dm² (1:2), pile height 4 mm.
Dyes: natural.
Colours (six): ivory, violet-brown, orange, dark brown, dark blue, green.
Finish: selvedges—no additional work; upper end— ivory plain weave, folded over on back and sewn down; lower end—0.5 cm violet-brown plain weave, folded over on front and sewn down; 1.5 cm ivory plain weave, folded over on back and sewn down; selvedges and lower end finished with 1.2 cm blue and brown plaited band, terminating at top in strings; 33 cm long tassels, attached.

Design and ornaments: septagonal central field, with five vertically arranged *erre* designs framed by three borders: main one carries the *dogajik* motif, vertical narrow borders the *saldat* motif and horizontal one the *syngyrma* design; one top border whose outline repeats the hexagon contains a chain of diamonds; at bottom broad *elem* panel with unidentified pattern of a *gapyrga*-type motif; side *elem* panel has white zigzag terminating at top in unpatterned white band.

First publication.
No near analogies identified.

75

76
Yomud asmalyk

140×89 cm

19th century
The Russian Museum, Leningrad.
No. KOB-166

Warp: grey wool, mixed with light brown, Z2S.
Weft: two shoots, very fine, dark brown wool, Z2S.
Pile: wool, Z2S.
Knot: symmetrical (SYI).
Knot density: 2,510 knots per dm^2 (1:2), pile height 3 mm.
Dyes: natural.
Colours (eight): dark red, orange, violet-brown, dark brown, dark blue, sky-blue, green, ivory.
Finish: selvedges—green wool, wrapped round two warps; upper end—violet-brown plain weave, folded over on back and sewn down; blue and red braided cord, woven in; red and green braided cords, attached to upper corners; lower end—violet-brown plain weave, folded over on back and sewn down; blue and red braided cord, woven in; sides and bottom finished with green and red plaited band having three tiers of multi-coloured tassels.
Design and ornaments: pentagonal central field divided into five vertical panels, each containing the *erre* design; colours of ground and *erre* design alternate (blue and red); three framing borders, with main one decorated with the *syrga* design and minor ones with the *sary ichyan* motif; in top border design changes into *giyak*-type geometrical motif.

First publication.
Analogies: Bogolyubov 1973, pl. 19.

76

77

77

Yomud asmalyk

127×70 cm

19th century
Museum of Ethnography, Leningrad.
No. 26-44/1

Warp: white wool, Z2S.
Weft: two shoots, white wool, Z2S.
Pile: wool, Z2.
Knot: symmetrical (SYI).
Knot density: 2,960 knots per dm^2 (1:2), pile height 3.5 mm.
Dyes: natural.
Colours (seven): violet-brown, bright red, dark yellow, mid-blue, greenish-blue, black, white.
Finish: selvedges—violet-brown wool, wrapped round two warps; red and brown plaited band, attached to side; upper end—green plain weave, folded over on front and sewn down; brown and sand-tinted plain weave, folded over on back and sewn down; lower end—3 cm white plain weave, folded over on back and sewn down; brown and crimson braided cord terminating in strings at top is attached to selvedges and lower end; multi-coloured three-tiered fringe attached to braided cord.

Design and ornaments: pentagonal central field with offset rows of large *dogajik* figures; central field framed by three borders; in top triangle their decoration changes into row of diamonds; main border decorated with the *koinekche nagshy* pattern, minor ones with a variation of the *khamtoz* motif; bottom *elem* panel decorated with small *dogajik* figures.

First publication.
Analogies: Museum of Ethnography, Leningrad, Nos. 26-43/1, 2 and 26-47/1, 2; The Hermitage, Leningrad, No. VT-737; Roberts 1981, pl. 63 (central field, several borders).

78
Yomud chuval

117×75 cm

19th century
The Russian Museum, Leningrad.
No. KOB-162

Warp: ivory wool, Z2S.
Weft: two shoots, brown wool, Z1.
Pile: wool, Z2S.
Knot: asymmetrical, open on right (ASII).
Knot density: 2,448 knots per dm^2 (1:1.9), pile height 4 mm.
Dyes: natural.
Colours (seven): violet-brown, red, yellow, mid-brown, dark blue, green, white.
Finish: selvedges—orange wool, wrapped round two warps; ends missing.
Design and ornaments: rectangular central field with 3 by 3 rows of *chuval göls* and secondary diamond-shaped figures; central field framed by three borders, main one decorated with a variation of the *tekbent* motif and minor ones with a variation of the *dogajik* design; top and side *elem* panels undecorated; broad bottom *elem* panel with three offset rows of small representations of dogs (?) and a stylized human figure.

First publication.
No near analogies identified.

78

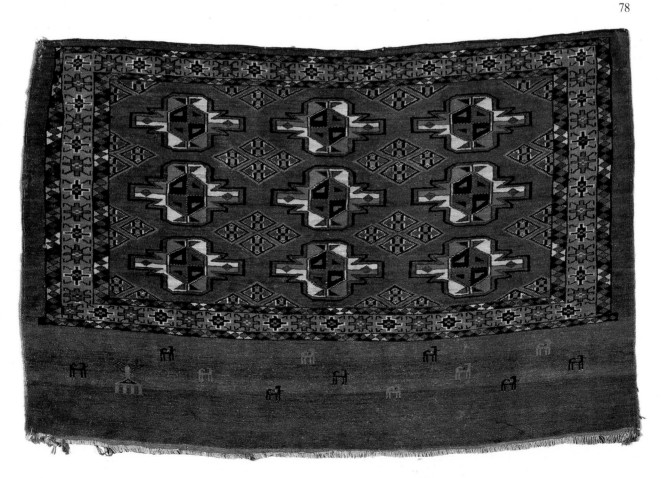

79

Yomud chuval

146×62 cm

Late 19th century
The Russian Museum, Leningrad.
No. KOB-178

Warp: grey wool, mixed with white, Z2S.
Weft: two shoots, very fine, white wool, mixed with brown; some strands twisted of white and red-dyed wool, Z2S.
Pile: wool, Z2S.
Knot: symmetrical (SYI).
Knot density: 2,400 knots per dm^2 (1:2.7), pile height 5 mm.
Dyes: natural and synthetic.
Colours (six): violet-brown, bright red, orange, dark blue, green, mid-blue.
Finish: selvedges—violet-brown wool, wrapped round two warps, back and face sewn together; upper end—green plain weave, folded over on back and sewn down; lower end—grey plain weave continues to form back of bag.
Design and ornaments: rectangular central field with 4 by 4 rows of small *chuval göls* and secondary *chemche* figures; central field framed by three borders with main one decorated with a variation of the *dogajik* pattern, and minor ones with the *sary ichyan*

design; side *elem* panel undecorated; top *elem* panel decorated with the *chetanak* design and bottom *elem* panel with rows of diamond-shaped figures.

First publication.
No near analogies identified.

79

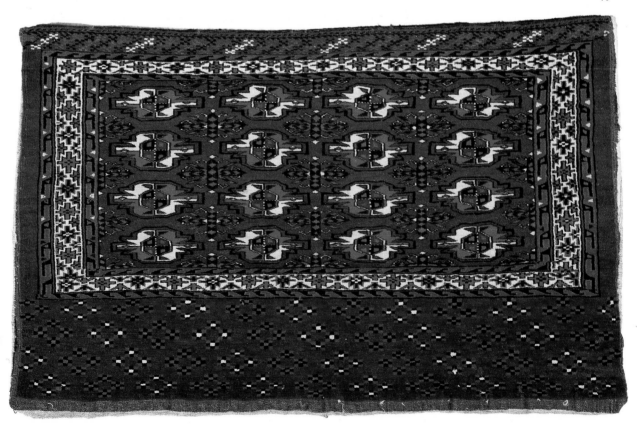

80
Yomud chuval

115×79.5 cm

19th century
Museum of Ethnography, Leningrad.
No. 26-59

Warp: white wool, Z2S.
Weft: two shoots, brown wool, Z1.
Pile: wool, Z2.
Knot: symmetrical (SYI), pile turned upwards.
Knot density: 3,444 knots per dm^2 (1:2), pile height 3 mm.
Dyes: natural.
Colours (eight): terracotta-red, bright red, orange, brown, dark blue, sky-blue, dark green, white.
Finish: selvedges—two pairs of warps, overcast with red wool, back and face sewn together; upper end—blue and brown plain weave, folded over on back and sewn down; red and green braided cords, attached to edge 24 cm from corners; lower end—red and white plain weave continues to form back of bag.
Design and ornaments: rectangular central field with 4 by 4 rows of small *chuval göls* and secondary *chemche* designs; central field framed by three borders, with main one decorated with unidentified design and minor ones with the *sary ichyan* motif; broad *elem* panels undecorated; top border has the *giyak* motif; upper *elem* panel decorated with representation of two bird's feet.

First publication.
Analogies: Gombos 1975, No. 44.

80

81

81
Yomud aina khalta

42×24 cm

Early 19th century
Museum of Ethnography, Leningrad.
No. 26-46

Warp: ivory wool, Z2S.
Weft: two shoots, brown wool, Z2.
Pile: wool, Z2.
Knot: symmetrical (SYI).
Knot density: 2,560 knots per dm^2 (1:1.6), pile height 2 mm (frayed).
Dyes: natural.
Colours (seven): cherry-red, orange, yellow, dark brown, mid-blue, blue-green, ivory.
Finish: selvedges—(left side, top) four pairs of warps, overcast with blue wool; (right side, bottom), cherry-red wool, wrapped round two warps; upper end—(left side) red and white plain weave, folded over on back and sewn down; lower end—(right side) red plain weave missing.

Design and ornaments: rectangular central field decorated with the *erre* design and enclosed in *khamtoz*-type border; *elem* panels undecorated.

First publication.
No analogies identified.

82

82
Yomud igsalik

80×77 cm

19th century
Museum of Ethnography, Leningrad.
No. 26-82/1

Warp: brown wool, Z2S.
Weft: two shoots, brown wool, mixed with grey, Z2S.
Pile: wool, Z2.
Knot: symmetrical (SYI).
Knot density: 2,030 knots per dm² (1:1.7), pile height 3 mm.
Dyes: natural.
Colours (seven): reddish-violet, orange, yellow, dark brown, light blue, green-blue, white.
Finish: selvedges—red-brown plain weave, folded over on back and sewn down; edge, hemmed with red and green woollen threads; red and brown braided loops attached to corners; upper end—four pairs of warps, overcast with green wool (weft thread looping only one warp thread); lower end— 'teeth' finished as selvedges; two tassels comprised of three four-sided braided cords with five-tier tassels of pile colours.
Design and ornaments: rectangular central field ornamented with the *erre*-type design and framed by three borders; main one carries the *saldat* design and minor ones the *chetanak* motif; narrow undecorated *elem* panels at sides and on top; edges of lower 'teeth' carry the *erre* motif; each 'tooth' contains a row of nests of triangles.

Published: Felkerzam 1914, pp. 90–81
Analogies: Moshkova 1970, fig. 62; Azadi 1975, No. 49; Mackie, Thompson 1980, pl. 83; Roberts 1981, pl. 64; Museum of Ethnography, Leningrad, No. 26-82/2.

83

83
Yomud igsalik

65×28 cm

Not later than mid-19th century
Museum of Ethnography, Leningrad.
No. 2017-3

Warp: white wool, mixed with grey, Z2S.
Weft: two shoots, fine, white wool, mixed with grey, Z2S.
Pile: wool, Z2S.
Knot: symmetrical (SYI).
Knot density: 2,960 knots per dm^2 (1:1.9), pile height 4 mm.
Dyes: natural.
Colours (seven): violet-brown, two shades of red, mid-brown, dark blue, green, ivory.
Finish: selvedges—plain weave folded back and oversewn with silk; upper end—red wool wrapped round warps; lower end—toothed, terminating in plain weave.
Design and ornaments: rectangular central field has rows of four-coloured zigzag bands with small crosses; central field enclosed by single vertical border decorated with the *giyak* design and three horizontal borders of which main one carries an unidentified design, and minor ones, the *saldat* motif; four bottom 'teeth' decorated with the same design as central field.

First publication.
No near analogies identified.

84 →
Yomud bukhcha

80×77 cm

19th century
The Russian Museum, Leningrad.
No. KOB-240

Warp: grey wool, mixed with some white and auburn, Z2S.
Weft: two shoots, very fine, white cotton twisted with pink silk, Z2S.
Pile: wool, lightly twisted, Z2S.
Knot: symmetrical (SYI).
Knot density: 2,720 knots per dm^2 (1:2.2), pile height 2.5 mm.
Dyes: natural.
Colours (eight): bright red, brown-red, orange, crimson, dark blue, sky-blue, green, ivory.
Finish: selvedges—(cloth) orange wool, wrapped round two warps; placed corner to corner and oversewn with orange wool; upper end—orange plain weave, hemmed along edge with blue and red silk; lower end—white plain weave, oversewn.
Design and ornaments: four triangles with identical pattern jointed at apexes; three broad borders with intermediate stripes decorated with the *giyak* and *alaja* motifs; main border carries row of diamonds outlined by a *giyak* band with unidentified crosslike ornament in the centre and at sides; enclosing borders carry the *syrga* motif.

First publication.
Analogies: Mackie, Thompson 1980, pl. 80; Jones, Boucher 1973, No. 40; Denny 1979, pl. 173; McMullan, Reichert 1970, pl. 67.

84

85

← 85
Yomud iolam

1,424×32 cm

19th century
Museum of Ethnography, Leningrad.
No. 26-3

Warp: ivory wool, Z2S.
Weft: white wool, Z3.
Pile: wool, silk, cotton, Z2.
Knot: symmetrical (SYI), single level.
Knot density: 4,950 knots per dm² (1:1.7), pile height 3 mm.
Dyes: natural.
Colours (eleven): orange-red, purple-red, pink, yellow, mid-brown, violet-brown, flesh-pink, blue, sky-blue (wool and silk) green, white (wool and cotton).
Finish: selvedges—brown wool, wrapped round four warps; ends—83 cm white plain weave with brocaded stripes; warps end in 60 cm long braided cords.
Design and ornaments: longitudinal bands with broad main one flanked by narrow minor ones; central band divided by transverse bands into row of panels with diverse designs based on principle of double mirror image; designs include the *gochak*, *kelle*, *chinar gül* and some unidentified motifs; axial lines of several panels filled with zoomorphic figures and the *ovadan* meander; minor flanking borders separated by multi-coloured zigzag; outer border carries a version of the *gochak* motif; inner border the *syngyrma* design.

First publication.
Analogies: Jones, Boucher 1973, No. 38 (some elements of central field).

86
Yomud iolam

212×44 cm

19th century
Museum of Ethnography, Leningrad.
No. 26-4

Warp: white wool, Z2S.
Weft: white, dark blue and dark red cotton, Z2S.
Pile: wool and cotton, lightly twisted, Z2S.
Knot: symmetrical, single level.
Knot density: 1,680 knots per dm² (1:1), pile height 2 mm (heavily frayed).
Dyes: natural.
Colours (eight): bright red, terracotta-red, yellow, brown, dark blue, sky-blue, dark green, white (cotton).
Finish: selvedges—bright red wool, wrapped round edge warps; ends—white plain weave with six brocaded stripes at one end; blue and red braided cords, with strings, woven into both edges; warps end in thin braided cords.
Design and ornaments: axial bands with broad main one and narrow minor ones; main band divided by transverse bands into row of panels which carry diverse designs based on principle of double mirror image, including the *kelle*, *charkh palak*, *gulyaidy* and *chinar gül* motifs; depicted at one end is a wedding caravan, a panel at the other end has rows of widely spaced small flowers; enclosing minor bands carry the *khamtoz* and *erik gül* designs separated by narrow multi-coloured zigzag.

Publications: Felkerzam 1914, pp. 44–45; Moshkova 1970, fig. 66.
Analogies: Azadi 1975, pl. 55; the Hermitage, Leningrad, No. VT-780.

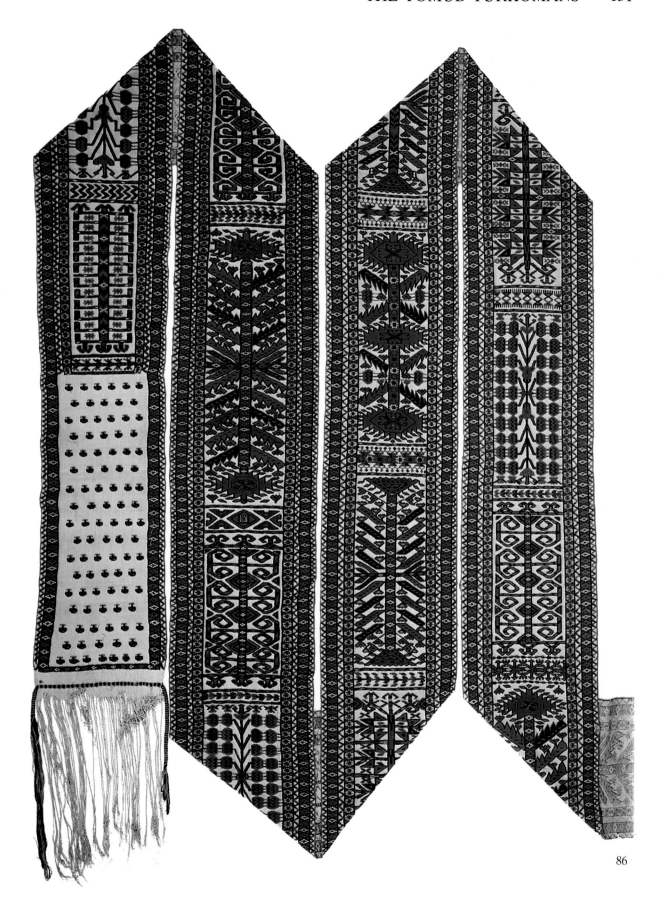

86

87, 88
Yomud iolam

1,562×49 cm

> 19th century
> Museum of Ethnography, Leningrad.
> No. 836-20

Warp: white wool, fine, Z2S.
Weft: white wool, very fine, Z2S.
Pile: wool and cotton, Z2S.
Knot: symmetrical, single level.
Knot density: 1,600 knots per dm^2 (1:1), pile height 3 mm.
Dyes: natural.
Colours (seven): violet-brown, light crimson, orange, mid-blue, sky-blue, dark green, white (cotton).
Finish: selvedges—no additional work; ends—warps end in thin tassels; red and blue braided cord 4 cm from edge.
Design and ornaments: a longitudinal row of panels with decoration arranged symmetrically with respect to the central longitudinal axis; basic motifs are variations of the *kelle* design: central pattern flanked by two bands, the outer one decorated with the *giyak* design, the inner with the *ovadan* meander; they are separated by a *zigzag*.

First publication.
No near analogies identified.

87

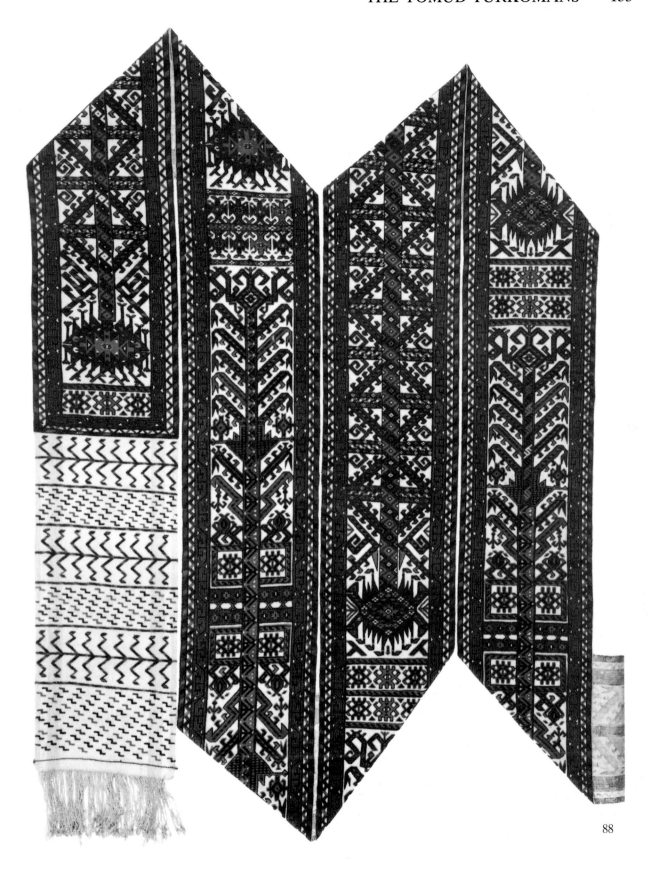

88

89
Ersari khali

207×134 cm

Mid-19th century
Museum of Ethnography, Leningrad.
No. 26-37

Warp: white wool, mixed with brown, Z2S.
Weft: thick, two shoots, white wool with some brown, Z1.
Pile: wool, Z2S.
Knot: asymmetrical, open on left (ASl).
Knot density: 728 knots per dm^2 (1:1), pile height 5 mm.
Dyes: natural.
Colours (seven): brick-red, light yellow, brown, mid-blue, sky-blue, green, white.
Finish: selvedges—red wool, wrapped round one warp; ends—22 cm striped (red, violet-red, light yellow, brown, sky-blue, white) plain weave.
Design and ornaments: rectangular central field with two rows of octagonal medallions decorated with the *onurga* design (old version, horizontal with two and half medallions per row); central field framed by two borders with a broad inner one carrying an *ai*-type design and a narrow outer one with the *sarkhalka* motif.

First publication.
No near analogies identified.

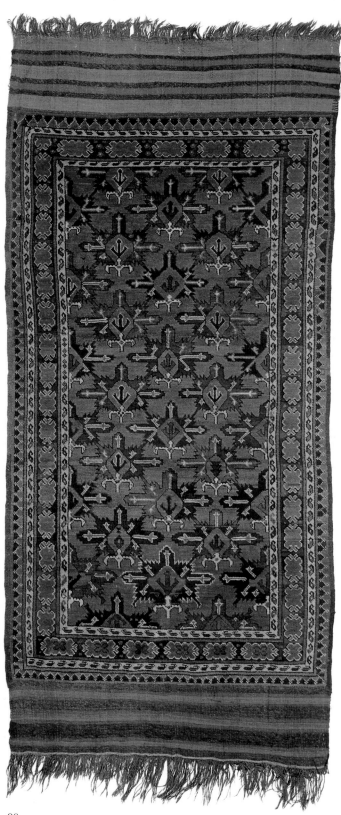

90
Ersari khali

290×138 cm

Second half 19th century
Museum of Ethnography, Leningrad.
No. 37-15

Warp: grey wool mixed with white and brown, Z2S.
Weft: two shoots, brown wool, mixed with white, Z2.
Pile: wool, Z2S.
Knot: asymmetrical, open on right (ASI, ASIII).
Knot density: 506 knots per dm² (1:1), pile height 8 mm.
Dyes: natural and synthetic (?).
Colours (nine): light red, light yellow, dark brown, sky-blue, bluish-grey, greenish-grey, mid-blue, light blue, white.
Finish: selvedges—four pairs of warps, overcast with brown wool; ends—32 cm red, sky-blue and brown plain weave; warps end in 8 cm long fringe at one end and 23 cm long fringe, at the other.
Design and ornaments: rectangular central field with diagonal rows of palmette-type figures; framed by four borders with main one carrying row of large figures resembling many-petalled flowers, two minor borders decorated with the *bodom* design and an outer border with the *saldat* motif in the Bashir variation.

First publication.
No near analogies identified.

91
Ersari khali

295×140 cm

Not later than mid-19th century
Museum of Ethnography, Leningrad.
No. 37-21

Warp: brown wool, mixed with grey and white, Z2S.
Weft: two shoots, brown wool, mixed with grey and white, Z1.
Pile: wool, Z2S.
Knot: asymmetrical, open on right (ASIII).
Knot density: 896 knots per dm^2 (1:1.2), pile height 10 mm.
Dyes: natural.
Colours (six): pinkish-red, yellow, light brown, dark blue, sky-blue, white.
Finish: selvedges—three pairs of warps, overcast with red wool; ends—10 cm striped plain weave; warps end in 20 cm long fringe.
Design and ornaments: rectangular central field decorated with *gerati* pattern and framed by five borders and two intermediate undecorated stripes; main border filled with intricate meander with toothed leaves, small floral motifs and large palmettes; outer border carries the *darak* motif; designs of other borders unidentified; main border extraordinarily broad for Turkoman carpets—its area twice as large as that of central field.

Published: Felkerzam 1914, pp. 68–69.

Analogies: though this type of decoration is common, no near analogies identified.

91

92

92
Ersari khali

219×134 cm

Not later than mid-19th century
Museum of Ethnography, Leningrad.
No. 37-23

Warp: fine grey wool, mixed with white, Z2S.
Weft: two shoots, brown wool, Z1.
Pile: wool, Z2S.
Knot: asymmetrical, open on right (ASII).
Knot density: 1,064 knots per dm² (1:1.4), pile height 6 mm.
Dyes: natural.
Colours (eight): brick red, orange, yellow, brown, dark blue, faded sky-blue, green, white.
Finish: selvedges—nine warps, overcast with red, blue and sky-blue wool; ends—sky-blue and red striped plain weave; warps end in 17 cm long fringe.
Design and ornaments: rectangular central field with eight offset vertical rows of large *bodom* figures; central field framed by two broad and two narrow borders; broad borders decorated with the Bashir variation of the *sary gyra* and *gozenek* designs, narrow ones with simpler variation of the *gozenek* design.

First publication.
No near analogies identified.

93 →
Ersari khali

255×154 cm

19th century
Museum of Ethnography, Leningrad.
No. 22694 "T"

Warp: grey wool, mixed with white. Z2S.
Weft: two shoots, brown wool. Z2S.
Pile: wool, Z2S.
Knot: asymmetrical, open on left (ASI).
Knot density: 1,472 knots per dm² (1:1.2), pile height 5–6 mm.
Dyes: natural.
Colours (ten): violet-brown, reddish-orange, yellow, brown, dark blue, sky-blue, olive-green, grey, pale mauve, white.
Finish: selvedges—three pairs of warps, overcast with olive-green wool; ends—red plain weave with brown stripes.
Design and ornaments: rectangular central field with 4 by 14 rows of *arabatchi göls* and secondary *chemche designs*; central field framed by three borders, main one decorated with a row of diamonds carrying geometrical design, minor ones with the *alaja* motifs; at bottom, inner minor border missing.

First publication.
No near analogies identified.

93

94

← 94
Ersari khali

300×200 cm

Second half 19th century
Museum of Ethnography, Leningrad.
No. 4710-4

Warp: grey wool, mixed with white, Z2S.
Weft: two shoots, red-dyed wool, twisted with brown, Z2.
Pile: wool, Z2S.
Knot density: 1,000 knots per dm^2 (1:1.5), pile height 3 mm.
Knot: asymmetrical, open on left (ASI).
Dyes: synthetic.
Colours (seven): brick-red, orange, yellow, brown, mid-blue, blue-green, white.
Finish: selvedges—three pairs of warps, overcast with brown wool; ends—16 cm red plain weave with blue stripes; warps end in fringe.
Design and ornaments: rectangular central field with 4 by 4 rows of *arabatchi göls* and secondary *gochak* designs, central field framed by main border with the *ovadan* pattern and two minor ones with the *giyak* design.

First publication.

Analogies: though carpets of the Kizil Ayak type are common, no near analogies identified.

95
Ersari khali

220×112 cm

19th century
Museum of Ethnography, Leningrad.
No. 37-24

Warp: white wool, mixed with grey, Z2S.
Weft: two shoots, red-dyed wool, Z1.
Pile: wool, Z2S.
Knot: asymmetrical, open on right (ASII), end row with symmetrical knots.
Knot density: 1,096 knots per dm^2 (1:1.6), pile height 5 mm.
Dyes: natural.
Colours (eight): violet-brown, bright red, yellow, dark brown, mid-blue, dark blue, greenish-blue, white.
Finish: selvedges—brown wool, wrapped round three warps; ends—6.5 cm striped plain weave, coloured as ground; warps end in fringe.
Design and ornaments: rectangular central field with 4 by 2 diagonal rows of large diamond-shaped medallions of the *khamtoz* type; entire surface of central field decorated with small *gosha kelle* flowers; central field framed by three borders; main border carries meander with *gochak* horns, minor ones the *saldat* motif.

First publication.

Analogies: though compositions of this type are common, no near analogies identified.

96
Ersari khali

292×140 cm

Second half 19th century
Museum of Ethnography, Leningrad.
No. 3180-1

Warp: white wool, mixed with grey, Z2S.
Weft: two shoots, red-dyed wool, Z2S.
Pile: wool, Z2S.
Knot: asymmetrical, open on left (ASI).
Knot density: 1,280 knots per dm² (1:1.2), pile height 5 mm.
Dyes: natural.
Colours (seven): red, bright red, yellow, orange, dark brown, blue, white.
Finish: selvedges and ends missing.
Design and ornaments: rectangular central field with large 2 by 4 straight lattice designs; diamond-shaped *khamtoz*-type figures in compartments; entire central field decorated with small *gosha kelle* flowers; at one end a panel with the *abr* design replaces two compartments with diamonds; entire composition framed by three borders with pattern identical to that of the band separating lattice compartments; main border decorated with a variation of the *gochak* design, minor ones with a variation of the *tekbent* pattern; remaining at one end is fragment of outer border carrying the *giyak* motif.

First publication.
Analogies: Azadi 1975, No. 7; Roberts 1981, No. 66.

97 →
Ersari khali (fragment)

625×260 cm

19th century
Museum of Ethnography, Leningrad.
No. 4712-1

Warp: white wool, mixed with grey, Z2S.
Weft: two shoots, grey wool, Z1.
Pile: wool, Z2S.
Knot: asymmetrical, open on right (ASII).
Knot density: 1,092 knots per dm² (1:1.7), pile height 5 mm.
Dyes: natural.
Colours (seven): brick-red, yellow, brown, dark blue, sky-blue, blue-green, white.
Finish: selvedges—four pairs of warps, overcast with red and sky-blue wool; ends—striped plain weave; warps end in fringe.
Design and ornaments: rectangular central field with repeat pattern of basic elements of *gerati* ornament, i.e. palmettes, toothed leaves and small flowered rosettes; central field framed by two main borders, three minor borders and four intermediate stripes; outer main border decorated with the *abr* design and inner with unidentified pattern of row of small stepped figures; minor borders decorated with the *erik gül* design and intermediate stripes with the *alaja* motif.

First publication.
No analogies identified.

97

98
Ersari namazlyk

185×110 cm

Before early 19th century
Museum of Ethnography, Leningrad.
No. 26-61

Warp: grey wool, Z2S.
Weft: two shoots, brown wool, Z1.
Pile: wool, Z2.
Knot: asymmetrical, open on right (ASII).
Knot density: 1,260 knots per dm^2 (1:1.4), pile height 6 mm.
Dyes: natural.
Colours (ten): red, pinkish-red, dark red, light yellow, orange-yellow, dark brown, mid-blue, sky-blue, dark green-blue, green.
Finish: selvedges—three pairs of warps overcast with red and blue wool; ends—striped plain weave; warps end in fringe; red and blue braided cord attached to one corner.
Design and ornaments: rectangular central field has pointed *mihrab* arch carrying small floral ornament of curved leaves on long slender winding stems; upper corners of arch terminate in large twinned *gochak* horn scrolls containing star-shaped *charkh palak* figures; central field framed by three borders, with main one carrying meander with leaves, similar to those of central field; one of extremely narrow minor borders carries the *alaja* motif and the other small triangles with apexes facing centre; ground of central field is white and of main border red; area of central field is twice that of borders.

Published: Felkerzam 1914, p. 68.
No analogies identified.

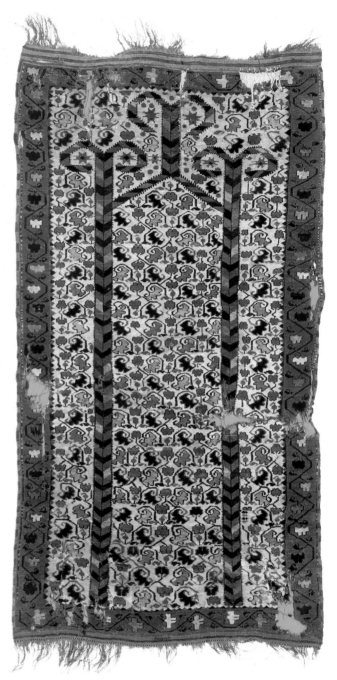

98

99
Ersari (Bashir) namazlyk

144×77 cm

19th century
Museum of Ethnography, Leningrad.
No. 4765-1

Warp: grey wool, mixed with white and brown, Z2S.
Weft: two shoots, fine, grey and light brown wool, lightly twisted, Z2S.
Pile: wool, Z2S.
Knot: asymmetrical, open on right (ASII).
Knot density: 1,008 knots per dm² (1:1.3), pile height 4.5–5 mm.
Dyes: natural.
Colours (six): red, beige, dark brown, dark blue, sky-blue, ivory.
Finish: three pairs of warps, overcast with red wool; ends—striped plain weave; warps end in fringe.
Design and ornaments: rectangular central field with pointed *mihrab* arch enclosing one more narrower arch decorated with seven large flowered rosettes; larger arch ornamented with rows of small flowers; central field framed by three borders; main one carries chain of triangles and minor ones the *giyak* design.

First publication.
No near analogies identified.

99

100

100
Ersari namazlyk

182×106 cm

First half 19th century
The Russian Museum, Leningrad.
No. KOB-259

Warp: grey wool, mixed with brown and white, Z2S.
Weft: two shoots, light brown wool, Z2S.
Pile: wool, Z2S.
Knot: asymmetrical, open on right (ASII).
Knot density: 2,160 knots per dm^2 (1:1.2), pile height 3 mm.
Dyes: natural.
Colours (eight): brick-red, light red, yellow, beige, brown, mid-blue, sky-blue, white.
Finish: selvedges—red and blue wool wrapped round one warp; ends—10 cm striped plain weave; warps end in 15 cm long fringe.
Design and ornaments: rectangular central field with pointed *mihrab* arch shows four large flowered rosettes and secondary figures in form of twinned, horizontally elongated, stylized leaves; arch formed by four rows of patterned bands with intermediate stripes carrying the *giyak* motif; three upper borders terminate in large twinned scrolls; two outer borders decorated with the *chinar gül* design, inner with a variation of the *darak* design, and the fourth with unidentified design of alternating figures in the shape of small flowered rosettes; flanking the arch in the corners of central field are stylized toothed leaves; upper portion of central field, above the arch, is rimmed by a chain of triangles; central field framed by three borders, main one carrying unidentified ornament of crosslike figures and minor ones a variation of the *darak* motif.

First publication.
Analogies: Mackie, Thompson 1980, pl. 95, Denny 1979, No. 70 (central field); Jones, Boucher 1973, pl. 33, 34; *The Ersari* 1975, pl. 1, 2, 3.

101
Ersari (Bashir) namazlyk

260×119 cm

19th century
Museum of Ethnography, Leningrad.
No. 37-17

Warp: grey wool, mixed with white, Z2S.
Weft: two shoots, wool, Z2S.
Pile: wool, Z2S.
Knot: asymmetrical open on right (ASII).
Knot density: 864 knots per dm^2 (1:1.6), pile height 8 mm.
Dyes: natural.
Colours (six): brick-red, yellow-auburn, dark brown, dark blue, sky-blue, white.
Finish: selvedges—two and three warps, oversewn with sky-blue and grey wool; ends—11 cm plain weave with blue, black, and sky-blue stripes on a red ground; warps end in 16 cm long fringe.
Design and ornaments: rectangular central field decorated with longitudinal bands; main one decorated with the *gerati* pattern, flanked by bands decorated with a row of stylized flowers on short stems; central field framed by three borders; main one has unidentified design consisting of chain of linked figures; inner border has meander with small flowers and outer one, two rows of triangles; central band of central field is on a red ground; flanking bands and main border are on a white ground.

First publication.
No near analogies identified.

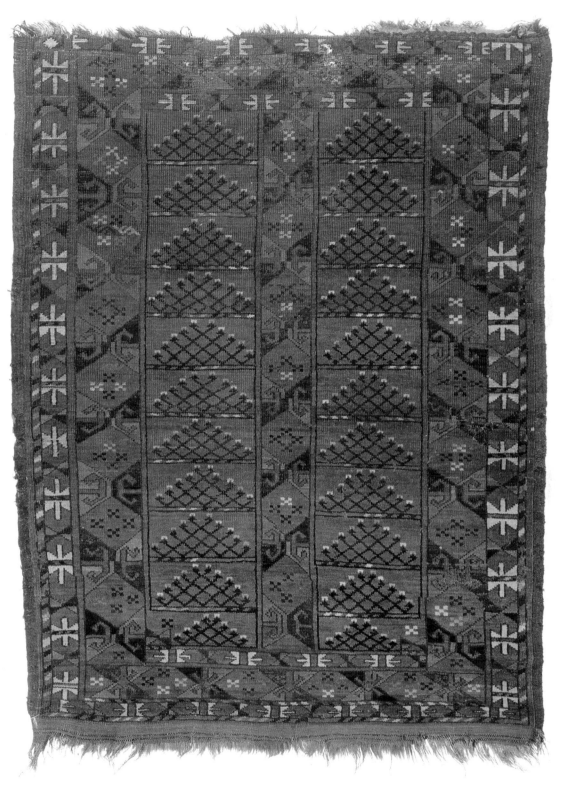

102

← 102
Ersari ensi

150×111 cm

19th century
Museum of Ethnography, Leningrad.
No. 22686 "T"

Warp: grey wool, mixed with white, Z2S.
Weft: two shoots, brown wool, Z2S.
Pile: wool and cotton, Z2S.
Knot: asymmetrical, open on right (ASII).
Knot density: 1,280 knots per dm^2 (1:1.3), pile
height 2 mm
Dyes: natural.
Colours (eight): violet-red, bright red, yellow, light
brown, dark brown, dark blue, green, white
(cotton).
Finish: selvedges—three pairs of warps, overcast
with brown wool; upper end—stitched with dark
brown wool (on eight warps); lower end—plain
weave of ground colour with two sky-blue stripes.
Design and ornaments: rectangular central field
divided into two vertical panels by broad band with
the *naldag*-type pattern; each panel divided into
eleven compartments with the *kush* motif arranged
as triangles; central field enclosed at top and bottom
in bands with the *darak* motif; entire composition
framed by three borders; main one decorated with
the same variation of the *naldag* pattern, another
with the *darak* motif, and outer one with the *giyak*
design; below, band decorated with the *giyak* design
between the *naldag* and *darak* borders; on the right
between them—broad unpatterned band; narrow
elem panels undecorated.

First publication.
No near analogies identified.

103
Ersari horse trapping (?)

120×87 cm

19th century
Museum of Ethnography, Leningrad.
No. 26-98

Warp: white wool, Z2S.
Weft: two shoots, different shades of brown wool
and white cotton in plain weave, Z2S.
Pile: wool, Z2.
Knot: symmetrical, side rows with asymmetrical
knots, open on right (on the left side), and open on
left (on the right side).
Knot density: 3,705 knots per dm^2 (1:2.5), pile
height 3 mm.
Dyes: natural.
Colours (eight): light terracotta-red, bright red,
orange-red, dark brown, mid-blue, sky-blue, green-
blue, white.
Finish: selvedges—one warp, wrapped with red and
brown wool; 1 cm wide blue and red plaited band,
attached to side; upper end—0.6 cm terracotta-red
plain weave, grey and white plaited band; warps end
in fringe firmly wrapped with multi-coloured wool;
lower end—plain weave with white cotton weft;
similar plaited band sewn on; blue and red braided
cord, woven in below; warps end in fringe.
Design and ornaments: pentagonal arch-shaped
central field with broad band of diamonds with four
pairs of small horns; small white panel carrying the
gochak motif at bottom; arch is formed by three
main bands and two minor ones; inner broad band
decorated with the *tekbent* design, central broad
band with a stalk from which scroll-like leaves
descend symmetrically on either side; outer broad
band carries the *khamtoz* design; in upper triangle
design of all borders changes into geometrical
diamond-shaped pattern; apex of arch is surmounted
by small pentagon with the *kelle* motif and small
bodom figures on a white ground; six rows of *bodom*
figures run parallel to lines in upper section of the
arch; four borders frame central composition; main
border decorated with the *atanak* design, two minor
borders carry the *sary ichyan* motif, outer border
carries the *giyak* motif; at top designs of all borders
change into diamond-shaped pattern.

Published: Felkerzam 1914, p. 52.
Analogies: Moshkova 1970, fig. 2; Azadi 1975,
pl. 42; Bernardout 1974, No. 15.

104
Ersari (Bashir) torba

130×45 cm

19th century
Museum of Ethnography, Leningrad.
No. 26-73

Warp: grey wool, mixed with white, Z2S.
Weft: two shoots, brown, pink and auburn wool, Z1.
Pile: wool and cotton, Z2, Z1.
Knot: asymmetrical, open on right (ASII), pile turned upwards.
Knot density: 1,066 knots per dm^2 (1:1.6), pile height 6 mm.
Dyes: natural.
Colours (nine): dark red, light red changing into auburn below, orange, beige, dark brown, mid-blue, sky-blue, green, white.
Finish: selvedges—pairs of warps, oversewn with red wool and attached to outer warp thread; upper end—red and white plain weave (cotton); 22 cm long multi-coloured fringe, attached.
Design and ornaments: rectangular central field with three *abr* (Chinese cloud) designs; framed by three borders, with main one decorated with *bodom* figures and minor ones with the *giyak* motif; *elem* panels decorated with the *kelle* design.

First publication.
Analogies: *The Ersari* 1975, No. 21; Thacher 1977, pl. 41.

105
Ersari (Bashir) torba

133×43 cm

19th century
Museum of Ethnography, Leningrad.
No. 26-66

Warp: grey wool, mixed white and brown, Z2S.
Weft: two shoots, light grey and brown (in middle) wool, Z2.
Pile: wool, lightly twisted, Z2S.
Knot: asymmetrical, open on right (ASII), pile turned upwards.
Knot density: 1,500 knots per dm^2 (1:1.4), pile height 5 mm.
Dyes: natural.
Colours (six): light red, yellow, brown, dark blue, sky-blue, white.
Finish: selvedges—two pairs of warps, overcast with red wool; pink and brown plaited band with strings at top, attached to side; upper end—striped plain weave, folded over on back and sewn down; pairs of twisted white and yellow threads at corners and in centre; lower end—grey plain weave, folded over on back and sewn down; 33 cm long multi-coloured fringe, attached.
Design and ornaments: rectangular central field decorated with *gerati* pattern; framed by two decorated and one plain border; main border carries the *charkh palak* motif, minor one the *sychan izy* design; top border decorated with the *govurdak* design.

Published: Felkerzam 1914, p. 75.
Analogies: Thacher 1977, pl. 40.

104

105

106

107

106
Ersari khurjun

103×47 cm

Late 19th century
Museum of Ethnography, Leningrad.
No. 7876-41

Warp: ivory wool, Z2S.
Weft: two shoots, red-dyed wool, twisted with brown, Z2S.
Pile: wool, Z2S.
Knot: asymmetrical, open on right (ASII).
Knot density: 1,600 knots per dm^2 (1:1), pile height 3 mm.
Dyes: natural.
Colours (seven): red, orange, brown, dark blue, mid-blue, light green, ivory.
Finish: selvedges—no additional work; back and face sewn together with brown woollen threads; ends—1 cm mid-blue plain weave continues to form back of bag; loops of brown woollen cords; multi-coloured tassels attached to corners.
Design and ornaments: rectangular central field consists of five vertical bands with alternating decoration of speckled *gochak* and *khamtoz* designs; central field framed by three borders with main one decorated with a variation of the *giyak* design and minor ones with another variation of the same design; at bottom broad *elem* panel with the *buynuz* design and on top two variations of the *khamtoz* motif.

First publication.
Analogies: Gombos 1975, No. 57.

107
Ersari asmalyk

168×64 cm

First half 19th century
The Russian Museum, Leningrad.
No. KOB-205

Warp: ivory wool, Z2S.
Weft: two shoots, grey wool, mixed with white and brown, Z1.
Pile: wool, Z2S.
Knot: asymmetrical, open on right (ASII), pile turned upwards.
Knot density: 1,643 knots per dm^2 (1:1.7), pile height 4 mm.
Dyes: natural.
Colours (five): cherry-red, orange, dark brown, dark blue, ivory.
Finish: selvedges—no additional work; 1.5 cm wide blue and red plaited band, attached to side; upper end—2 cm red plain weave with green brocaded stripe, folded over on front and sewn down; 1 cm ivory plain weave, folded over on back and sewn down; lower end—0.5 cm red plain weave followed by 0.5 cm ivory plain weave, folded over on front and sewn down; 1 cm ivory plain weave, folded over on back and sewn down; remains of dark blue woollen fringe knotted on four warps.
Design and ornaments: rectangular central field with two large star-shaped rosettes, filled with complex design and secondary *kejebe* figures; central field framed by three borders, main one decorated with unidentified design and minor ones with the *chakmak* and *alaja* motifs; *elem* panels undecorated; top border with the *giyak* design.

First publication.
No near analogies identified.

108
Arabatchi (Ersari group) torba

125×50 cm

> 19th century
> Museum of Oriental Art, Moscow.
> No. 1265 III

Warp: ivory wool, mixed with white and brown, Z2S.
Weft: two shoots, ivory wool, twisted with camel hair, Z2S.
Pile: wool, Z2S.
Knot: asymmetrical, open on right (ASII).
Knot density: 2,170 knots per dm^2 (1:2.2), pile height 4 mm.
Dyes: natural.
Colours (seven): violet-brown, bright red, beige, dark brown, dark blue, bluish-green, ivory.
Finish: selvedges—violet-brown wool, wrapped round three warps; upper end—0.5 cm bluish-green plain weave, folded over on front and sewn down; 1.5 cm ivory plain weave, folded over on back and sewn down; lower end—auburn plain weave, cut; remains of fringe of pile colours knotted on two pairs of warps.
Design and ornaments: rectangular central field with large star-shaped rosette in the middle, flanked by halves of such rosettes and with secondary *kejebe* designs; central field framed by four vertical and three horizontal borders; main border decorated with the *charkh palak* design, minor borders with the *chetanak* motif; inner vertical border has the *gochak* design; *elem* panels are undecorated; top border has the *giyak* design.

First publication.
Analogies: see No. 110.

109
Arabatchi (Ersari group) asmalyk

123×88 cm

> 19th century
> Museum of Ethnography, Leningrad.
> No. 87-7

Warp: grey wool, Z2S.
Weft: two shoots, camel hair and white cotton, Z2S.
Pile: wool, silk, Z2S.
Knot: asymmetrical, open on left (ASI).
Knot density: 2,016 knots per dm^2 (1:1.3), pile height 10 mm.
Dyes: natural and synthetic (?).
Colours (ten): violet-brown, brick-red, crimson, yellow, salmon (silk), beige, dark blue, blue-green, white, dark brown.
Finish: selvedges—violet-brown wool, wrapped round two warps; upper end—1 cm grey plain weave, with two braided cords (one—blue and

108

109

yellow, the other—red and violet-brown) woven in, folded over on front and sewn down; 3 cm similar plain weave, folded over on back and sewn down; lower end—5 cm striped grey plain weave; warps end in 23 cm long fringe; multi-coloured fringe knotted on four warps.

Design and ornaments: pentagonal central field with 6 by 4 rows of two-headed birds; three schematic representations of *yurts* or *kejebe* tents in upper triangle; central field framed from sides and below by five borders; main border has changing design of vertically disposed *gochak* motifs and of camel caravan with wedding tents; flanking borders decorated with the Ersari variation of the *sary gyra* design, guard borders carry unidentified geometrical design; top border composed of two rows of small diamonds with small crosses between them; at bottom, narrow border with the *giyak* pattern.

Published: Bogolyubov 1973, ill. 24.

No analogies identified.

110
Arabatchi (Ersari group) torba

138×62 cm

19th century
The Russian Museum, Leningrad.
No. KOB-203

Warp: grey wool, mixed with brown and white, Z2S.
Weft: two shoots, camel hair and white cotton, lightly twisted, Z2S.
Pile: wool, Z2S.
Knot: asymmetrical, open on left (ASIII).
Knot density: 2,160 knots per dm^2 (1:1.7), pile height 5 mm.
Dyes: natural.
Colours (six): violet-brown, orange, dark brown, mid-blue, green, white.
Finish: selvedges—brown wool wrapped round two warps; upper end—0.5 cm red plain weave with three additional red and blue wefts passed over two warps; folded over on front and sewn down; ivory plain weave, folded over on back and sewn down; lower end—red plain weave, cut; remains of green and violet-brown woollen fringe knotted on five warps.
Design and ornaments: rectangular central field with large central star-shaped rosette flanked by halves of similar rosettes and with secondary *kejebe*-type figures; central field framed by three borders with intermediate *alaja* stripes; main border decorated with the *charkh palak* design and minor borders with the *chakmak* motif; narrow bottom *elem* decorated with small *dogajik* figures; side *elem* panel undecorated; top stripe carries the *alaja* motif.

First publication.
Analogies: Mackie, Thompson 1980, No. 55.

110

111
Arabatchi (Ersari group) chuval (?)

147×90 cm

First half 19th century
Museum of Ethnography, Leningrad.
No. 2018-4

Warp: grey wool, Z2S.
Weft: two shoots, white cotton and camel hair, lightly twisted, Z2S.
Pile: wool and silk, Z2S.
Knot: asymmetrical, open on left (ASIII).
Knot density: 1,428 knots per dm^2 (1:1.2), pile height 6–7 mm.
Dyes: natural.
Colours (nine): violet-brown, crimson, pink (silk), orange, yellow, dark brown, dark blue, sky-blue, ivory.
Finish: selvedges—violet-brown wool, wrapped round four warps; upper end—1 cm violet-brown plain weave; orange and blue braided cord, woven in; folded over on front and sewn down; ivory plain weave, folded over on back and sewn down; lower end—violet-brown plain weave missing.
Design and ornaments: rectangular central field with 4 by 4 rows of small *chuval göls* and secondary *chemche* designs; central field framed by three borders with main one decorated with the *gochak* motif and two minor ones with the *chakmak* design; vertically disposed on the inner side are another two borders decorated with the *sarkhalka* and *chetanak* designs; broad bottom *elem* panel with ten large *kelle* figures; narrow side *elem* panel undecorated; top stripe carries the *giyak* pattern.

First publication.
No near analogies identified.

112
Arabatchi (Ersari group) asmalyk

146×62 cm

Not later than mid-19th century
The Russian Museum, Leningrad.
No. KOB-187

Warp: ivory wool, mixed with grey, Z2S.
Weft: two shoots, very fine, white cotton and camel hair, lightly twisted, Z2S.
Pile: wool and silk, Z2S.
Knot: asymmetrical, open on left (ASIII).
Knot density: 2,100 per dm^2 (1:1.7), pile height 3.5 mm.
Dyes: natural.
Colours (ten): violet-brown, crimson (silk), orange-red, orange, yellow, brown, dark blue, sky-blue, green, white.
Finish: selvedges—violet-brown wool, wrapped round three warps; upper end—red plain weave, trimmed with orange-green supplementary weave; ivory plain weave, folded over on back and sewn down; lower end—violet-brown plain weave and ivory plain weave, cut; remains of multi-coloured fringe knotted on four warps.
Design and ornaments: rectangular central field with four small diamond-shaped medallions and five pairs of secondary old-version *kejebe* figures; central field framed by three borders and *alaja* intermediate stripes; main border decorated with the *darak* pattern, minor ones with the *chakmak* design; bottom *elem* panel has the *khamtoz* motif; top *elem* panel has 13 *kelle* heads; narrow side *elem* panel undecorated; top stripe has the *giyak* design.

First publication.
No near analogies identified.

111

112

113
Chodor torba

134×48 cm

19th century
The Russian Museum, Leningrad.
No. KOB-224

Warp: grey wool, mixed with white, Z2S.
Weft: two shoots, white cotton and camel hair, lightly twisted, Z2S.
Pile: wool and silk, Z2S.
Knot: asymmetrical, open on right (ASII), pile turned upwards.
Knot density: 2,280 knots per dm² (1:1.6), pile height 5 mm.
Dyes: natural.
Colours (nine): violet-brown, orange-red, crimson (silk), crimson-red, yellow, brown, dark blue, sky-blue, white.
Finish: selvedges—violet-brown wool, wrapped round two warps; upper end—violet-brown plain weave with red and blue plaited band, folded over on front and sewn down; plain weave of similar colour followed by ivory plain weave, folded over on back and sewn down; lower end missing.
Design and ornaments: rectangular central field with two complete and two half Chodor *göls* (late variation) and secondary half Chodor *göls* (in another variation); central field framed by three borders and *alaja* intermediate stripes; main border decorated with the *kojanak* design and minor ones with the *chakmak* motif; bottom *elem* panel decorated with 13 *kelle* figures; narrow side *elem* panel undecorated; top band with the *giyak* design.

First publication.
Analogies: Denny 1979, colour pl. 22.

113

114

← 114
Chodor khali (fragment)

176×100 cm

Last third 19th century
Museum of Ethnography, Leningrad.
No. 36-9

Warp: grey wool, mixed with white, Z2S.
Weft: two shoots, white cotton, Z2.
Pile: wool, Z2S.
Knot: asymmetrical, open on right (ASII).
Knot density: 1,472 knots per dm^2 (1:1.4), pile height 4 mm.
Dyes: natural and synthetic.
Colours (six): violet-brown, bright red, yellow, dark blue, dark green, white.
Finish: selvedges—six pairs of warps, overcast with brown wool; ends—11 cm brown and white plain weave; warps end in 20 cm long fringe.
Design and ornaments: rectangular central field with diagonal diamond lattice pattern formed of thin zigzags; compartments contain diagonal rows of Chodor *göls*; central field framed by three borders with three *giyak* intermediate stripes; main border decorated with the *ovadan* motif and minor ones with the *khamtoz* design; broad *elem* panel carries offset rows of *dogajik* figures.

First publication.
Analogies: Mackie, Thompson 1980, No. 51; Jones, Boucher 1973, Nos. 23–24.

115
Chodor khali

441×223 cm

19th century
Museum of Ethnography, Leningrad.
No. 4753-5

Warp: grey wool, Z2S.
Weft: two shoots, light brown wool and white cotton, untwisted, Z2.
Pile: wool, Z2S.
Knot: asymmetrical, open on left (ASI).
Knot density: 1,400 knots per dm^2 (1:1.8), pile height 4 mm.
Dyes: natural.
Colours (seven): violet-brown, red, yellow, brown, blue-green, green, white.
Finish: selvedges—two pairs of warps, oversewn with brown wool; ends—10 cm white and brown plain weave; warps end in fringe.
Design and ornaments: rectangular central field with diagonal diamond lattice design formed by thin broken lines with small flowers; compartments contain diagonal rows of Chodor *göl* motifs; central field framed by three borders with four *gozenek* intermediate stripes; main border decorated with meander of *dogajik* motifs, minor borders with unidentified geometrical pattern; top and bottom *elem* panels decorated with eight brown and red stripes carrying *dogajik* figures.

First publication.
Analogies: Jones, Boucher 1973, Nos. 23–24.

115

116
Kashgarlyk Uzbek namazlyk

290 × 100 cm

First half 19th century
Museum of Ethnography, Leningrad.
No. 16-206

Warp: white cotton, Z2S.
Weft: three shoots, brown wool, Z1.
Pile: wool, lightly twisted, Z2S.
Knot: asymmetrical, open on right (ASIV).
Knot density: 896 knots per dm^2 (1:1.1), pile height 5 mm.
Dyes: natural.
Colours (seven): faded red, brick-red, yellow, dark brown, mid-blue, sky-blue, white.
Finish: selvedges—red wool, wrapped round two warps; ends (sides)—1 cm white plain weave; warps end in fringe.
Design and ornaments: rectangular central field divided into seven broad panels with *mihrab* arches; each arch has three designs: straight stemmed stalk with flowers and leaves, stalk with toothed leaves and rows of small flowered rosettes; central field framed by one border containing row of squares, each filled with quatrefoil; narrow undecorated border on top.

First publication.
Analogies: S. Reed, *Oriental Rugs and Carpets*, London, 1967, p. 10.

116

117
Uzbek giliam

289×43 cm

Late 19th century
Museum of Ethnography, Leningrad.
No. 36-24

Warp: grey wool, mixed with white and brown, Z2S.
Weft: two shoots, grey wool, mixed with white and brown, Z1.
Pile: wool, Z2S.
Knot: asymmetrical, open on left (ASI).
Knot density: 484 knots per dm^2 (1:1), pile height 10 mm.
Dyes: natural and synthetic.
Colours (six): brick-red, yellow, brown, mid-blue, sky-blue, white.
Finish: selvedges—no additional work; 2 cm wide plaited band attached to side; ends—20 cm striped plain weave; warps end in 40 cm long fringe.
Design and ornaments: rectangular central field with 2 by 5 rows of large stepped medallions filled with diamond and horn-shaped design; secondary diamonds with compartmented filling and toothed outline; central field framed by three borders, with main one decorated with pattern of diamonds and triangles of the *kerege nuska* design and minor ones with oblique strokes.

First publication.
No near analogies identified.

118
Uzbek Turkman khali

330×145 cm

Late 19th century
Museum of Ethnography, Leningrad.
No. 362-21

Warp: grey wool, mixed with brown, Z2S.
Weft: two shoots, grey wool mixed with brown, Z2S.
Pile: wool, Z2S.
Knot: asymmetrical, open on right (ASIV).
Knot density: 864 knots per dm^2 (1:1.2), pile height 3 mm.
Dyes: natural and synthetic.
Colours (nine): red, brown-red, mauve-red, pink-ivory, brown, green, sky-blue, grey-green, white.
Finish: selvedges—three warps, overcast with wool of pile colours; ends—10 cm brown, red, blue and white striped plain weave; warps end in fringe.
Design and ornaments: rectangular central field with 2 by 8 rows of *kalkan nuska* medallions and secondary *gochak* figures; central field framed by three borders; main one decorated with the *kerege nuska*-type motif and minor ones with meander that the Turkomans call the *sarkhalka* motif.

First publication.
Analogies: Moshkova 1970, fig. 30 (central field).

117

118

119
Uzbek giliam

284×148 cm

Late 19th century
Museum of Ethnography, Leningrad.
No. 34-25

Warp: ivory and light brown wool, Z2S.
Weft: two shoots, light brown wool, Z2S.
Pile: wool, Z2S.
Knot: asymmetrical, open on left (SI).
Knot density: 576 knots per dm^2 (1:1), pile height 7 mm.
Dyes: natural and synthetic.
Colours (nine): brick-red, bright red, dark yellow, beige, brown, dark blue, sky-blue, light grey, white.
Finish: selvedges—three pairs of warps, overcast with blue wool; ends—14 cm brown plain weave with blue and red stripes; warps end in 37 cm long braided cords.
Design and ornaments: rectangular central field with *kerege nuska* diagonal lattice design; framed by three borders, with main one consisting of a chain of diamonds and triangles and minor ones decorated with the *chetanak* design.

First publication.
No near analogies identified.

119

120

120
Uzbek (?) giliam

186×97 cm

Late 19th century
Museum of Ethnography, Leningrad.
No. 34-27

Warp: grey wool, mixed with white and brown, Z2S.
Weft: one shoot, brown wool, Z1.
Pile: wool, Z2S.
Knot: asymmetrical, open on left (SYI).
Knot density: 840 knots per dm^2 (1:1.1), pile height 3 mm.
Dyes: natural and synthetic.
Colours (seven): cherry-red, bright red, yellow, light brown, mid-blue, green, greenish-blue.
Finish: selvedges—three pairs of warps, overcast with red, yellow and sky-blue wool; ends—3 cm plain weave; warps end in fringe; overcast with coloured woollen threads and terminating in tassels.
Design and ornaments: rectangular central field with 3 by 10 rows of small geometrical rosettes, framed by four borders, with main one having the *gochak* design and three minor ones an unidentified geometrical pattern.

First publication.
No analogies identified.

121

121
Uzbek julkhyrs

207×115 cm

19th century
Museum of Ethnography, Leningrad.
No. 24-25

Warp: grey wool, mixed with white and brown, Z2S.
Weft: one shoot, dark brown wool, Z2S.
Pile: wool, very thick strands, Z2.
Knot: symmetrical, single level.
Knot density: 252 knots per dm^2 (1:1.3), pile height 15 mm.
Dyes: natural with synthetic pink.
Colours (seven): brick-red, pink, dark brown, yellow, sky-blue, dark blue, blue-green.
Finish: selvedges—no additional work; carpet stitched together from four bands; ends—grey plain weave, folded over on back and sewn down.
Design and ornaments: rectangular central field with 2 by 3 rows of *kuchkor shokh* diamonds and secondary star-shaped rosettes; framed by broad band carrying the *kuchkorak* design, row of speckles and narrow undecorated stripe along the edge.

First publication.
No analogies identified.

122 →
Uzbek tent-door lambrequin

114×87 cm

Late 19th century
Museum of Ethnography, Leningrad.
No. 36-26:

Warp: white wool, mixed with brown, Z2S.
Weft: two shoots, light brown wool, Z2.
Pile: wool, Z2S.
Knot: asymmetrical, open on left (ASI).
Knot density: 1,353 knots per dm^2 (1:1.3), pile height 3 mm.
Dyes: synthetic.
Colours (eleven): red, pink, yellow, brown, mid-blue, sky-blue, blue-green, grey-green, grey, mauve, white.
Finish: selvedges—two warps, overcast with blue, white, yellow and red wool; lower ends—white fabric and fringe, sewn onto plain weave; transverse band finished as selvedges; woven open-worked fringe with tassels, attached to lower edge.
Design and ornaments: design arranged in bands with row of *kuchkor shokh* medallions on transverse band and figures consisting of four pairs of scroll horns on arms.

First publication.
No analogies identified.

123
Uzbek chinakap

60×33 cm

19th century
Museum of Ethnography, Leningrad.
No. 1435-53/2

Warp: ivory wool, lightly twisted, Z2S.
Weft: one shoot, ivory wool, Z1.
Pile: wool, Z2S.
Knot: symmetrical, single level.
Knot density: 176 knots per dm^2 (1:1), pile height
10 mm.
Dyes: natural and synthetic.
Colours (seven): pink-red, yellow, brown, mid-blue,
bluish-green, grey, ivory.
Finish: selvedges—no additional work, edges sewn
with brown wool; upper end—2 cm ivory plain
weave, folded over and sewn down; lower end—
sewn as selvedges; remains of long multi-coloured
tassels.
Design and ornaments: decorated surface divided
into upper rectangular and bottom triangle; in upper
portion the *pakhta* design is arranged in three rows
to form angles, with intermediate undecorated
stripes; in the bottom portion six *pakhta* figures; top
stripe carries row of triangles.

First publication.
No analogies identified.

123

124

Uzbek napramach

90×43 cm

Late 19th century
Museum of Ethnography, Leningrad.
No. 24-33

Warp: brown wool, mixed with grey, Z2S.
Weft: two shoots, brown wool, lightly twisted, Z2S.
Pile: wool, Z2S.
Knot: asymmetrical, open on right (ASII).
Knot density: 810 knots per dm^2 (1:1.1), pile height 16 mm.
Dyes: natural and synthetic.
Colours (seven): light-red, yellow, brown, mid-blue, sky-blue, bluish-green, green.
Finish: selvedges (top and bottom of the piece)— 0.5 cm unworked plain weave; ends—grey plain weave with red and blue stripes, folded over on back and sewn down.
Design and ornaments: rectangular central field with three octagonal medallions with centralized *charkh palak* motif, framed by border with speckles; horizontal bands carry small zigzag figures; vertical bands carry *kuchkorak* horns.

First publication.
Analogies: Moshkova 1970, fig. 21.

125

Uzbek Turkman (?) tent bag

90×43 cm

First half 19th century
Museum of Ethnography, Leningrad.
No. 362-22

Warp: white wool, mixed with brown, Z2S.
Weft: two shoots, grey wool, mixed with brown, Z2S.
Pile: wool, Z2S.
Knot: asymmetrical, open on right (ASII), pile turned upwards.
Knot density: 2,070 knots per dm^2 (1:2), pile height 3 mm.
Dyes: natural.
Colours (six): cherry-red, orange, brown, blue, green, ivory.
Finish: selvedges—brown and orange wool, wrapped round two pairs of warps; upper end— 1.5 cm red and green plain weave, folded on front and sewn down; 1 cm ivory plain weave, folded on back and sewn down; lower end—1.5 cm red and ivory plain weave, folded back and sewn down; remains of multi-coloured fringe knotted on four warps.
Design and ornaments: rectangular central field with offset rows of *kuchkor shokh* medallions; framed by three borders, with main one decorated with the *darak* pattern and minor ones with chain of triangles; broad undecorated side stripes and row of speckles on top.

First publication.
No analogies identified.

124

125

126
Karakalpak wedding curtain
(detail)

149×212 cm

First half 19th century
Museum of Ethnography, Leningrad.
No. 8230-3

Warp: white wool and white cotton, Z2S.
Weft: one shoot, white wool, Z2S.
Pile: wool, Z2S.
Knot: symmetrical, single level.
Knot density: 1,080 knots per dm² (1:1.2), pile height 2 mm.
Dyes: natural and synthetic.
Colours (thirteen): cherry-red, bright red, light red, yellow, brown, mid-blue, sky-blue, grey, grey-green, green, violet, ivory, white.
Finish: selvedges—no additional work; sewn of twelve bands; ends—edges cut and unsewn; transverse band sewn onto edge; short wrapped tassels and red fringe sewn onto seam; red fringe, attached.
Design and ornaments: twelve bands with variations of the *muiiz* design; each band is between two types of guard borders, one having zigzags, the other scrolls.

First publication.
Analogies: Museum of Ethnography, Leningrad. No. 23801 "T".

126

127

127, 128
Karakalpak karshin

94×32 cm

19th century
Museum of Ethnography, Leningrad.
No. 5111-137

Warp: brown wool, mixed with white, Z2S.
Weft: brown wool, Z1.
Pile: wool, cotton, Z3-5S; silk, lightly twisted, Z1.
Knot: symmetrical (SYI).
Knot density: 2,090 knots per dm^2 (1:1.5), pile height 4 mm.
Dyes: natural.
Colours (nine): bright red, yellow, two shades of brown, olive-green, mid-blue, sky-blue (silk), ivory, white (cotton).
Finish: selvedges (top and bottom of the piece)—red wool, wrapped round two warps; upper end—2 cm red and brown plain weave, folded over on front and sewn down; 2 cm brown plain weave, folded over on back and sewn down; lower end—7 cm brown and red plain weave; 1 cm, folded over on back and sewn down.
Design and ornaments: rectangular central field with 6 by 2 rows of *göl*-type medallions and secondary *muiiz* figures; framed by narrow border of short oblique strokes.

First publication.
Analogies: see No. 131.

129
Karakalpak khurjin

112×41 cm

Late 19th or early 20th century
Museum of Ethnography, Leningrad.
No. 22827 "T"

Warp: grey wool, mixed with white and brown, Z2S.
Weft: two shoots, light brown wool, Z1.
Pile: wool, Z2S.
Knot: asymmetrical, open on right (ASII).
Knot density: 1,352 knots per dm^2 (1:2), pile height 6 mm.
Dyes: synthetic.
Colours (six): orange red, magenta, cherry-red, yellow, dark blue, white.
Finish: selvedges—two warps, overcast with red wool, back and face braided together; upper end— 1 cm red plain weave on front; 4 cm magenta plain weave, folded over on back; brown loops knotted in along edge; lower end—white plain weave continues to form back of bag.
Design and ornaments: rectangular central field ornamented with *muiiz* motif and framed by three borders, main one with the *darak* pattern and minor ones with short oblique strokes; broad bottom *elem* panel decorated with a variation of *muiiz* design; stripe with row of small horns on top.

First publication.
No analogies identified.

130
Karakalpak napramach

77×41 cm

Late 19th century
Museum of Ethnography, Leningrad.
No. 24-34

Warp: grey wool, Z2S.
Weft: one shoot, grey wool, Z1.
Pile: wool, Z2S.
Knot: symmetrical (SYI).
Knot density: 2,636 knots per dm^2 (1:2), pile height 8 mm.
Dyes: synthetic and natural.
Colours (five): red, yellow, dark brown, green, white.
Finish: selvedges (top and bottom of the piece)— two pairs of warps, overcast with red wool; ends— 10 cm grey and brown fabric, folded over on back and sewn down.
Design and ornaments: rectangular central field with four large Chodor *muiiz* rosettes and secondary triangles.

First publication.
Analogies: Moshkova 1970, fig. 26.

129

130

131

131
Karakalpak karshin

120×36 cm

> 19th century
> Museum of Ethnography, Leningrad.
> No. 7128-13

Warp: brown wool, Z2S.
Weft: one shoot, grey wool with brown, Z2S.
Pile: wool, Z2S.
Knot: symmetrical (SYI).
Knot density: 1,440 knots per dm² (1:1.1), pile height 5 mm.
Dyes: natural and synthetic.
Colours (five): red, orange, dark brown, dark blue, white.
Finish: selvedges—eight warps, oversewn with orange wool; ends—1 cm brown plain weave, folded over on back and sewn down.
Design and ornaments: rectangular central field with diagonal rows of octagonal *göl*-type medallions and secondary *muiiz* figures; framed by stripe with diamond-shaped ornament.

First publication.
Analogies: see No. 127.

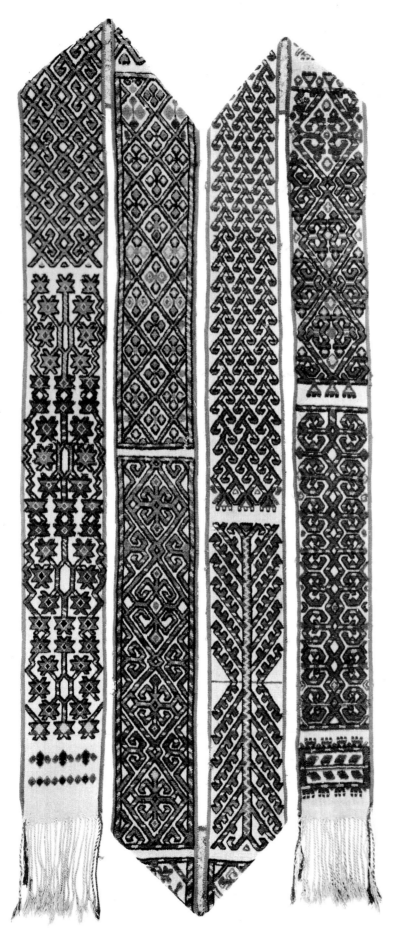

132
Karakalpak baskur

540×25 cm

Early 20th century
Museum of Ethnography, Leningrad.
No. 23691 "T"

Warp: white wool, Z2S.
Weft: one shoot, grey wool, mixed with white, Z2S.
Pile: wool, Z2S.
Knot: symmetrical, single level.
Knot density: 1,088 knots per dm² (1:1), pile height 5 mm.
Dyes: natural.
Colours (five): bright red, yellow, mid-brown, grey-brown, light grey.
Finish: selvedges—no additional work; ends—white plain weave; warps end in 25 cm long tassels.
Design and ornaments: band of eight panels interior design of which is based on double mirror image principle; five panels decorated with variations of the *muiiz* horn pattern, one with star-shaped *charkh palak* design, another with *gapyrga*-type motif and another with geometrical diamond lattice.

First publication.
No near analogies identified.

132

133
Kirghiz (Ferghana Valley) kilem

363×214 cm

Second half 19th century
Museum of Ethnography, Leningrad.
No. 34-36

Warp: grey wool, mixed with white and brown, Z2S.
Weft: two shoots, grey wool, Z2S.
Pile: wool, lightly twisted, Z2S.
Knot: asymmetrical, open on right (ASII).
Knot density: 576 knots per dm^2 (1:1), pile height 11–12 mm.
Dyes: natural.
Colours (seven): brick-red, yellow, violet-brown, sky-blue, green, black, white.
Finish: selvedges—three warps overcast with violet-brown wool; ends—20 cm striped plain weave; warps end in fringe.
Design and ornaments: rectangular central field decorated with small *orus kochot* floral design; central field framed by four borders; main one decorated with row of short stems with three flowers each, two borders carry a *darak*-type motif; inner border decorated with a variation of the *tumarcha* design.

First publication.
No analogies identified.

134
Khydyrsha Kirghiz kilem

300×158 cm

Late 19th century
Museum of Ethnography, Leningrad.
No. 36-5

Warp: grey wool, mixed with white and brown, Z2S.
Weft: two shoots, light brown wool, mixed with white, lightly spun, Z2S.
Pile: wool, Z2S.
Knot: asymmetrical, open on left (ASI).
Knot density: 576 knots per dm^2 (1:1), pile height 13 mm.
Dyes: natural.
Colours (six): violet-brown, red, yellow, dark brown, sky-blue, white.
Finish: selvedges—four warps, overcast with wool of pile colours; ends—grey plain weave; braided cord, woven in; warps end in long thick tassels.
Design and ornaments: rectangular central field with rows of small *toguz dobo* flowered rosettes, framed by two borders and outer narrow speckled stripes; broad border decorated with a *mashaty*-type diamond-shaped design, narrow border, with the *tumarcha* motif.

First publication.
No analogies identified.

135
Kirghiz (Ferghana Valley) kilem

285×148 cm

19th century
Museum of Ethnography, Leningrad.
No. 34-26

Warp: two threads of white cotton, twisted with one of white wool, Z2S.
Weft: one shoot, white and brown wool, Z2S.
Pile: wool, Z2S.
Knot: asymmetrical, open on left (ASI).
Knot density: 832 knots per dm^2 (1:1.2), pile height 4 mm.
Dyes: natural.
Colours (six): red, beige-pink, brown, mid-blue, bluish-green, white.
Finish: selvedges—three warps, overcast with red wool; ends—5 cm red and green plain weave; warps end in fringe.
Design and ornaments: rectangular central field with six compartments filled with floral pattern in the form of three stems with flowers and *mashaty* leaves; central field framed by three borders with inner border decorated with row of five-petalled *it taman* flowers which is similar to the ornamentation of intermediate stripes of central field; main and outer borders decorated with variations of the *tumarcha* motif.

First publication.
No analogies identified.

134

135

136
Khydyrsha Kirghiz kilem
248×137 cm

Second half 19th century
Museum of Ethnography, Leningrad.
No. 34-32

Warp: white wool, mixed with brown, Z2S.
Weft: one shoot, white wool, mixed with brown, Z2S.
Pile: wool, Z2S.
Knot: asymmetrical, open on left (ASI).
Knot density: 576 knots per dm^2 (1:1), pile height 6 mm.
Dyes: natural and synthetic.
Colours (seven): red, pink, yellow, brown, mid-blue, sky-blue, green.
Finish: selvedges—two pairs of warps overcast with brown wool; ends—5 cm brown plain weave pink and brown braided cord, woven in; warps end in 15 and 54 cm long tassels.
Design and ornaments: rectangular central field with three large stepped medallions and secondary triangles adjacent to vertical borders; central field framed by three borders, main one decorated with row of horn-shaped *kaikalak* figures, inner minor with chain of small flowers, outer border with row of *tumarcha* triangles.

First publication.
No analogies identified.

136

137
Khydyrsha Kirghiz kilem

272×142 cm

Late 19th century
Museum of Ethnography, Leningrad.
No. 14-38

Warp: ivory wool, Z2S.
Weft: one shoot, ivory wool, Z1.
Pile: wool, Z2S.
Knot: asymmetrical, open on left (ASI).
Knot density: 768 knots per dm^2 (1:1.3), pile height 7 mm.
Dyes: natural and synthetic.
Colours (seven): red, pink, yellow, brown, beige, blue, white.
Finish: selvedges—three pairs of warps overcast with wool of pile colours; ends—4 cm plain weave; warps end in cords.
Design and ornaments: rectangular central field with delicate diamond lattice; small *mashaty* flowered rosettes in compartments and at intersections of lattice lines; central field framed by four borders with main one decorated with the *omurtka*-type diamond-shaped design; inner border decorated with the *yulduz* design and outer band with the *tumarcha* motif; row of speckles on edge.

First publication.
No analogies identified.

137

138

138
Khydyrsha Kirghiz kilem

179×100 cm

Second half 19th century
Museum of Ethnography, Leningrad.
No. 5118-1.

Warp: brown wool, fine, Z2S.
Weft: two shoots, grey and brown wool, mixed with ivory, Z2S.
Pile: wool, Z2S.
Knot: symmetrical (SYl).
Knot density: 1,232 knots per dm^2 (1:1.7), pile height 4 mm.
Dyes: natural and synthetic.
Colours (seven): pink-red, cherry-violet, yellow, brown, dark blue, green-blue, white.
Finish: selvedges—brown wool, wrapped round edge warps (later); ends—blue-striped red plain weave with frayed edge.
Design and ornaments: rectangular central field with 3 by 7 straight lattice design; stem with three flowers and long leaves in each compartment; central field framed by two borders with two *giyak* intermediate stripes; broad inner border decorated with row of stepped geometrical figures; narrow outer band has row of triangles separated by broken *iirek* line.

First publication.
No analogies identified.

139
Kirghiz kilem

450×140 cm

Second half 19th century
Museum of Ethnography, Leningrad.
No. 23004 "T"

Warp: white cotton, Z5S.
Weft: two shoots, light brown wool, Z2S.
Pile: wool, Z2S.
Knot: asymmetrical, open on left (ASI).
Knot density: 704 knots per dm^2 (1:1.5), pile height 4–5 mm.
Dyes: natural.
Colours (seven): two shades of red, yellow, brown, mid-blue, green, ivory.
Finish: selvedges—four warps, overcast with red wool; ends—12 cm striped plain weave; warps end in 12 cm long fringe.
Design and ornaments: rectangular central field with transverse rows of diverse large figures: three pairs of oblongs enclosed in small horns and filled with pattern of small horns, five rows of geometrical-type rosettes in groups of three and six rows of *dogdan*-type medallions; central field framed by three borders, with main border decorated with floral motif, inner minor one with chain of small diamonds and outer with small squares.

First publication.
No analogies identified.

139

140

140
Kirghiz eshik tysh

162×95 cm

Late 19th century
Museum of Ethnography, Leningrad.
No. 14-33

Warp: brown wool, twisted with white, Z2S.
Weft: one shoot, very thick, grey wool, mixed with brown, Z2S.
Pile: wool, Z2S.
Knot: asymmetrical, open on left (ASI).
Knot density: 572 knots per dm^2 (1:1.2), pile height 7–8 mm.
Dyes: natural and synthetic.
Colours (seven): red-pink, red, brown, grey-brown, dark blue, sky-blue, white.
Finish: selvedges—no additional work; upper end—grey-brown plain weave; warp ends braided into thick four-sided strings; lower end—4 cm grey plain weave; warps end in fringe.
Design and ornaments: rectangular central field with broad longitudinal band ending before reaching transverse border; decorated with two rows of *kuchkorak* designs; diamond-shaped *kaikalak* rosette lower down, beneath band; central field framed, at bottom and along sides, by two borders; broad inner border decorated with a variation of the *kuchkorak* design, narrower outer one with the *tumarcha* motif.

First publication.
No analogies identified.

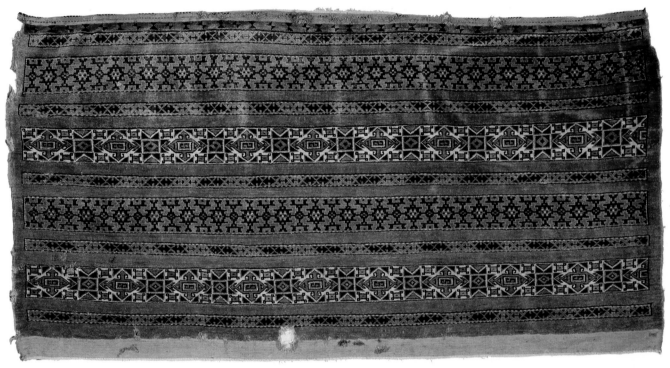

141

141
Kirghiz kap

213×108 cm

Before mid-19th century
Museum of Ethnography, Leningrad.
No. 14-127

Warp: grey wool, mixed with white, lightly twisted, Z2S.
Weft: two shoots, light brown wool, Z1.
Pile: wool, Z2S.
Knot: asymmetrical, open on right (ASII), pile turned upwards.
Knot density: 960 knots per dm² (1:1), pile height 5 mm.
Dyes: natural.
Colours (seven): red, orange-red, violet-red (almost identical with ground colour), mid-blue, dark blue, bluish-green, white.
Finish: selvedges—red wool, wrapped round two warps; upper end—3 cm red plain weave; sky-blue braided cord, woven in; white plain weave, folded over on back and sewn down; blue and red braided cord, woven in along edge; lower end—7 cm red plain weave; white plain weave, folded over on back and sewn down.
Design and ornaments: rectangular central field with four broad and five narrow transverse bands; broad bands decorated with *gurbaka* and *mashaty*-type patterns; narrow bands decorated with chain of diamond-shaped figures filled with geometrical design; top stripe carries the *tumarcha* motif.

First publication.
Analogies: Museum of Ethnography, Leningrad. No. 14-33.

142
Kirghiz kosh jabyk

77×77 cm

Second half 19th century
Museum of Ethnography, Leningrad.
No. 14-77

Warp: light brown wool, mixed with some white, Z2S.
Weft: one shoot, light brown wool, mixed with white, Z2S.
Pile: wool, Z2S.
Knot: asymmetrical, open on right (ASII).
Knot density: 896 knots per dm^2 (1:1.1), pile height 7 mm.
Dyes: natural.
Colours (five): brick-red, yellow, brown, blue, ivory.
Finish: selvedges—no additional work; upper end—3.5 cm brown plain weave, 2 cm folded over on back and sewn down; woven fringe attached to edge; plaited strings attached to corners; lower end—brown plain weave, cut.
Design and ornaments: rectangular central field with three vertical *choidysh* figures; framed by two borders with variations of the *tumarcha* design.

Published: Antipina 1962, fig. 48.
No analogies identified.

142

143
Kirghiz (Ferghana Valley)
bashtyk

50×50 cm

Early 20th century
Museum of Ethnography, Leningrad.
No. 6371-7

Warp: white wool, mixed with brown, Z2S.
Weft: one shoot, white wool, mixed with brown, Z1.
Pile: wool, Z2.
Knot: asymmetrical, open on right (ASII).
Knot density: 700 knots per dm² (1:1.3), pile height 5 mm.
Dyes: synthetic.
Colours (six): brick-red, pink-red, flesh-pink, dark brown (dyed), mid-blue, white.
Finish: selvedges—no additional work; ends—1 cm light brown plain weave, folded back and sewn down.

Design and ornaments: rectangular central field with stepped *kaikalak* rosette; framed by border with *it taman* design and two narrow undecorated borders.

First publication.
Analogies: Moshkova 1970, fig. 36; *Transactions* 1968, table VII, No. 1; Antipina 1962, fig. 36.

143

144

144
Kirghiz kosh jabyk

90×82 cm

Late 19th or early 20th century
Museum of Ethnography, Leningrad.
No. 6371-9

Warp: white wool, twisted with brown, Z2S.
Weft: one shoot, brown wool, Z1.
Pile: wool, Z2S.
Knot: asymmetrical, open on right (ASII).
Knot density: 896 knots per dm² (1:1.1), pile height 4 mm.
Dyes: synthetic.
Colours (eight): crimson-red, pink-red, yellow, brown, mid-blue, sky-blue, blue-green, white.
Finish: selvedges—no additional work; ends—1 cm grey plain weave, folded over on back and sewn down; 12 cm long dark blue fringe, attached; 50 cm long 4-sided braided strings, attached to corners.

Design and ornaments: rectangular central field with straight *orus kochot* lattice design (one row displaced); framed by three borders; main one with the *ilmek* design; minor ones, undecorated.

First publication.
Analogies: *Transactions* 1968, Table VIII, N6.1, Fig. 48.

145

145
Kirghiz kosh jabyk

102×77 cm

Late 19th or early 20th century
Museum of Ethnography, Leningrad.
No. 6371-11

Warp: brown wool, mixed with auburn and white, Z2S.

Weft: one shoot, grey-brown and red-dyed wool, Z2S.

Pile: wool, Z2S.

Knot: asymmetrical, open on left (ASl).

Knot density: 616 knots per dm^2 (1:1.3), pile height 6 mm.

Dyes: natural.

Colours (seven): bright red, orange, red-brown, mid-brown, yellow-green, mid-blue, white.

Finish: selvedges—no additional working; upper end—2 cm brown plain weave, folded over on back and sewn down; lower end—2 cm red-grey plain weave; plain edge; 19 cm long warp ends, open; blue open worked fringe with tassels, sewn on sides and top.

Design and ornaments: rectangular central field with 3 by 6 rows of horizontally elongated *toguz dobo* flowered rosettes with diamonds between them; central field framed by two borders, broad inner one decorated with the *it taman* design surrounded by speckles, and outer narrow one with the *tumarcha* design.

First publication.
No analogies identified.

146
Kazakh saddle covering

101×66 cm

1950s
Museum of Ethnography, Leningrad.
No. 6037-1

Warp: brown sheep and goat wool, Z2S.
Weft: one shoot, grey wool, mixed with white and brown, Z2S.
Pile: wool, Z1.
Knot: asymmetrical, open on left (ASl).
Knot density: 864 knots per dm^2 (1:1.5), pile height 4 mm.
Dyes: synthetic.
Colours (six): brick-red, pink-red, yellow, brown, blue, white.
Finish: selvedges—no additional work; ends (slanting line)—1 cm brown plain weave, folded over on back; open-work plaited band; tassels sewn on around entire piece.
Design and ornaments: octagonal central field with three *kuchkorak* figures; larger central one contained in irregular hexagon flanked by figures of similar type; surrounded by broken lines forming an open octagon; central field framed by stripe with a *kuchkorak*-type pattern and two broad undecorated borders.

First publication.
No analogies identified.

146

147

147
Kazakh giliam

240×135 cm

Late 19th century
Museum of Ethnography, Leningrad.
No. 23793 "T"

Warp: grey wool, Z2S.
Weft: two shoots, grey wool, mixed with brown, Z1.
Pile: wool, Z2S.
Knot: asymmetrical, open on right (ASII).
Knot density: 780 knots per dm^2 (1:1.1), pile height 7 mm.
Dyes: natural and synthetic.
Colours (eight): brick-red, red-pink, yellow, faded orange, brown, blue, green, white.
Finish: selvedges—three pairs of warps, overcast with brown wool; ends—30 cm brown, beige and red striped plain weave, unsewn.
Design and ornaments: rectangular central field with large diagonal lattice design; compartments carry diamonds composed of numerous triangles; central field framed by three borders, main one decorated with the *umurtka* pattern; flanked by minor borders with small crosslike figures.

First publication.
No analogies identified.

148

148
Kazakh giliam

185×145 cm

1950s
Museum of Ethnography, Leningrad.
No. 6978-2

Warp: white cotton, Z2S.
Weft: one shoot, white wool, Z5.
Pile: wool, Z1.
Knot: symmetrical (SYI).
Knot density: 1,360 knots per dm^2 (1:1.2), pile height 8 mm.
Dyes: synthetic.
Colours (nine): bright red, orange, cherry-red, khaki, blue, violet, green, black, white.
Finish: selvedges—two warps, oversewn with red wool; ends—1.5 cm red plain weave; warps end in 9 cm long fringe.
Design and ornaments: rectangular central field with 3 by 5 rows of medallions having *muiiz* motifs and secondary figures, similar but of simpler form; central field framed by three borders, main one decorated with triangles containing complex horn motif; minor borders carry chain of small horn scrolls.

First publication.
Mass production.

149
Kazakh baskur

1,322×27 cm

Late 19th or early 20th century
Museum of Ethnography, Leningrad.
No. 22818 "T"

Warp: white and red cotton, Z2S.
Weft: white cotton, Z2S.
Pile: wool, Z2S.
Knot: symmetrical, single level.
Knot density: 1,280 knots per dm^2 (1:1.2), pile height 3 mm.
Dyes: natural and synthetic.
Colours (four): orange, yellow, dark brown, blue.
Finish: selvedges—red wool, wrapped round three warps; ends—plain weave; warps braided into 100 cm long, four-sided cords.
Design and ornaments: band divided into nine panels with pile-woven pattern alternating with tapestry design; pile-woven pattern based on principle of double mirror image and composed of variations of horn-shaped designs and *tumarcha* motifs.

First publication.
Analogies: though there are many bands of this type, no near analogies identified.

149

150
Baluch floor rug

140×80 cm

19th century
Museum of Ethnography, Leningrad.
No. 25-3

Warp: white wool, Z2S.
Weft: two shoots, brown wool, lightly spun and twisted, Z2S.
Pile: wool, Z2S.
Knot: asymmetrical, open on left (ASIII).
Knot density: 1,216 knots per dm^2 (1:1.1), pile height 6 mm.
Dyes: natural.
Colours (six): red, cherry-red, violet-brown, dark brown, beige, white.
Finish: selvedges—4 pairs of warps, overcast with brown wool; ends—19 cm striped plain weave; warps end in 10 cm long fringe.
Design and ornaments: rectangular central field with floral design based on principle of double mirror image with stalk with large palmette-type leaves; central field framed by three borders and four intermediate stripes with speckles; inner minor border decorated with row of star-shaped figures; main border with row of triangles whose apexes end in stylized bird heads; outer minor border with design of small spear-shaped black and white figures.

First publication.
Analogies: Black, Loveless 1976, Nos. 4, 40.

150

151
Baluch main carpet

222×90 cm

19th century
Museum of Ethnography, Leningrad.
No. 25-6

Warp: white wool, Z2S.
Weft: two shoots, light brown wool, Z2S.
Pile: wool, lightly twisted, Z4S.
Knot: asymmetrical, open on right (ASII), uneven knotting.
Knot density: 896 knots per dm^2 (1:1.1), pile height 4 mm.
Dyes: natural.
Colours (six): brick-red, orange, dark blue, sky-blue, green, white.
Finish: selvedges—four pairs of warps, oversewn with brown wool; ends—12 cm embroidered plain weave; warps end in fringe.
Design and ornaments: rectangular central field with overall floral and zoomorphic design of six vertical stalks with flowers and leaves; minute representations of birds (two versions) and *bodom* figures set between leaves; central field framed by three borders and three intermediate stripes with speckles; main border decorated with complex composition of trefoils and pairs of *tumar* amulets; minor ones decorated with two rows of nested triangles with scrolls.

First publication.
No near analogies identified.

151

152
Baluch rug

82×45 cm

> 19th century
> Museum of Ethnography, Leningrad.
> No. 25-13

Warp: ivory wool, Z2S.
Weft: two shoots, very fine, brown wool, Z2S.
Pile: wool, Z3.
Knot: asymmetrical, open on left (ASl).
Knot density: 2,728 knots per dm² (1:1.4), pile height 2 mm.
Dyes: natural.
Colours (seven): cherry-red, orange-red, dark brown, dark blue, sky-blue, green, white.
Finish: selvedges—orange edge warp threads, Z6, strengthened by red braided cord; ends—brown plain weave, cut.
Design and ornaments: rectangular central field with diagonal rows of *bodom* figures framed by three borders and four intermediate stripes with speckles; main border decorated with geometrical design consisting of oblongs linked by crosslike figures, minor ones decorated with rows of triangles.

First publication.
No near analogies identified.

152

153
Baluch rug

83×67 cm

19th century
Museum of Ethnography, Leningrad.
No. 25-15

Warp: ivory wool, Z2S.
Weft: two shoots, very fine, brown wool, lightly spun, Z2S.
Pile: wool, Z2S.
Knot: asymmetrical, open on left (ASI).
Knot density: 2,016 knots per dm² (1:1.1), pile height 2 mm.
Dyes: natural.
Colours (six): cherry-red, orange-red, dark brown, black, dark blue, white.
Finish: selvedges cut.
Design and ornaments: rectangular central field with straight 3 by 4 lattice design filled with zoomorphic pattern based on principle of double mirror image; central field framed by three borders, with main one decorated with chain of diamonds; minor ones carry meander with geometrized floral design.

First publication.
Analogies: McMullan, Reichert 1970, No. 73.

153

154

← 154
Baluch rug

52×54 cm

Second half 19th century
Museum of Ethnography, Leningrad.
No. 8700-4

Warp: ivory wool, Z2S.
Weft: two shoots, dark brown wool, lightly twisted, Z2S.
Pile: wool, Z2S.
Knot: asymmetrical, open on right (ASII).
Knot density: 1,856 knots per dm^2 (1:1.8), pile height 3 mm (frayed).
Dyes: natural.
Colours (eight): red, orange-red, dark brown, violet-brown, dark blue, light blue, black, white.
Finish: selvedges—three warps, overcast with brown wool (two edge threads are dark brown); ends—black plain weave, cut.
Design and ornaments: rectangular central field with diagonal lattice design filled with large floral patterns; central field framed by three borders, main one with meander with geometricized floral motifs, minor ones carry two rows of small spear-shaped figures of contrasted colouring; four intermediate stripes with speckles.

First publication.
No analogies identified.

155
Baluch tent bag

140×78 cm

19th century
Museum of Ethnography, Leningrad.
No. 25-5

Warp: white wool, Z2S.
Weft: two shoots, fine, brown wool, lightly twisted, Z2S.
Pile: wool, Z2S.
Knot: asymmetrical, open on left (ASI).
Knot density: 1,200 knots per dm^2 (1:1.3), pile height 5 mm.
Dyes: natural.
Colours (eight): violet-red, red, dark brown, beige, mid-blue, white, sky-blue, yellow.
Finish: selvedges—two pairs of warps, overcast with black wool, back and face sewn together; upper end—17 cm brocaded plain weave; 1 cm folded over on back and sewn down; lower end—red and black striped plain weave, turned over onto back.
Design and ornaments: rectangular central field with representation of plant on thick stalk with broad toothed leaves; framed by three borders and four intermediate stripes with speckles; main border decorated with pattern of long slender plants with leaves; inner minor border with two rows of spear-shaped figures of contrasting colours; outer minor border with two rows of irregular pentagons resembling bird heads.

First publication.
No near analogies identified.

155

The Salor Turkomans

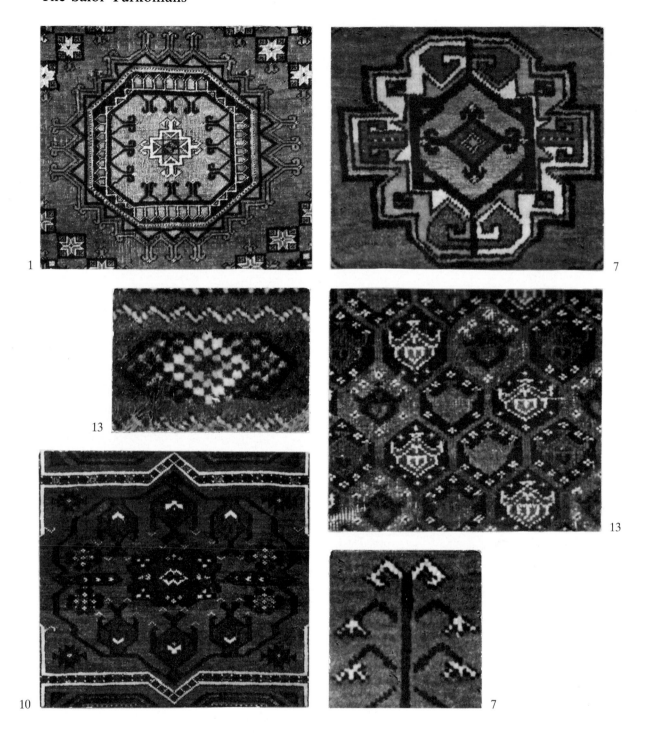

1

7

13

13

10

7

The Saryk Turkomans

15

24

17

17

17

17

27

24

26

The Tekke Turkomans

The Yomud Turkomans

45

55

58

66

70

66

77, 67

76

66

The Ersari Turkomans

94

The Chodor Turkomans

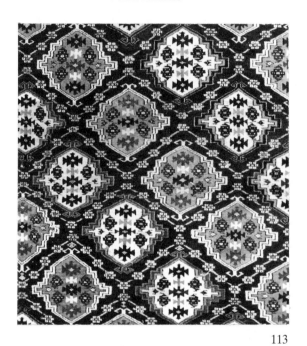

113

The Arabatchi Turkomans

109

109, 111

The Uzbeks

118

The Karakalpaks

126

128

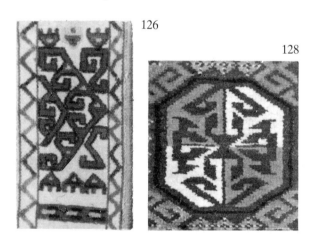

The Kirghiz

139   139

The Kirghiz

136

140

The Kazakhs

The Baluch of Central Asia

153

149

151

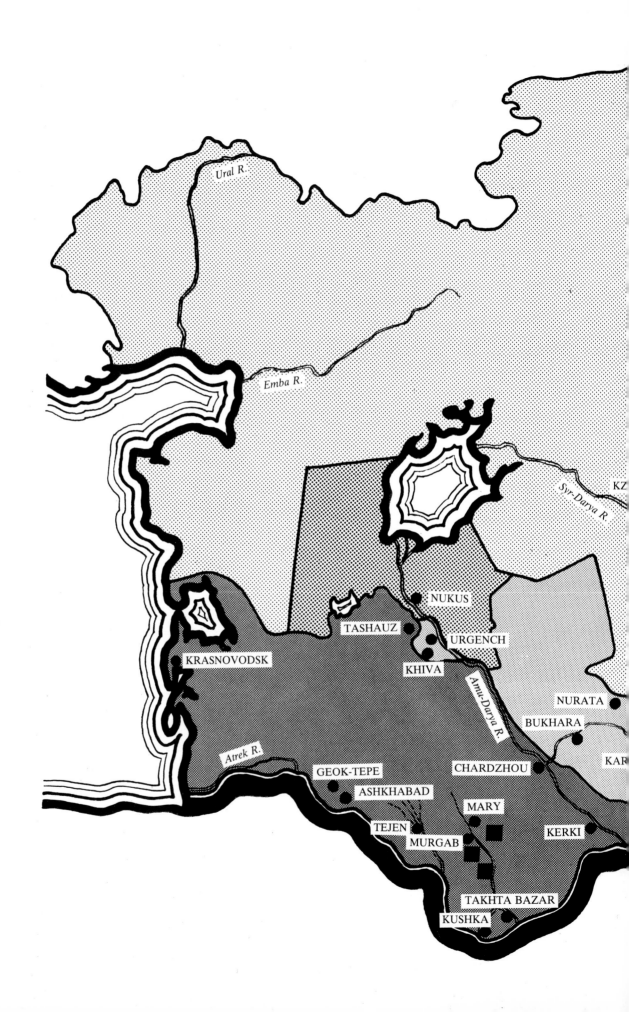

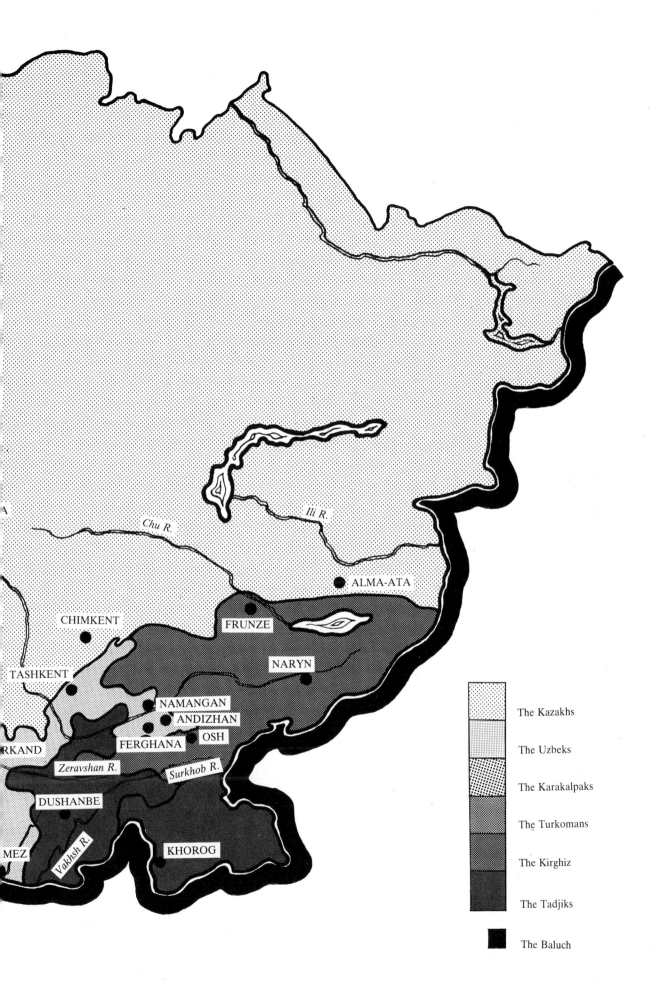

Chu R.

Ili R.

● ALMA-ATA

CHIMKENT
●

● FRUNZE

TASHKENT
●

NARYN
●

NAMANGAN
●
ANDIZHAN
●
● OSH
FERGHANA
●

RKAND

Zeravshan R.

Surkhob R.

DUSHANBE
●

MEZ

Vakhsh R.

KHOROG

The Kazakhs

The Uzbeks

The Karakalpaks

The Turkomans

The Kirghiz

The Tadjiks

The Baluch

Adamov, A. K., *Soviet Carpets and Their Export*, Moscow, Leningrad, 1934 [А. К. Адамов, *Советские ковры и их экспорт*, Москва, Ленинград, 1934]

Andrews, P. A., "The Türkmen Tent", *Hali*, vol. 4, No. 2, 1981, pp. 108–117

Antipina, K. I., *Specific Features of the Material Culture and Art of the Southern Kirghiz*, Frunze, 1962 [К. И. Антипина, *Особенности материальной культуры и искусство южных киргизов*, Фрунзе, 1962]

Antipina, K. I., "Pile Weaving", in: *Popular Decorative and Applied Art of the Kirghiz. Transactions of the Kirghiz Archaeological and Ethnographical Expedition*, vol. 5, Frunze, 1971, pp. 59–78 [К. И. Антипина, "Ворсовое ткачество, в кн.: *Народное декоративно-прикладное искусство киргизов. Труды киргизской археолого-этнографической экспедиции*, т. 5, Фрунзе, 1971, с. 59–78]

Azadi, S., "Asmalyk. Eine neu entdeckte Gattung", *Turkoman Studies I*, London, 1980, pp. 172–181

Azadi, S., *Turkoman Carpets and the Ethnographic Significance of Their Ornaments*, Fishguard, 1975

Benardout, R. B., *Catalogue of Turkoman Weaving Including Beluch*, London, 1974

Benardout, R. B., *Tribal and Nomadic Rugs*, London, 1976

Beresneva, L. G., *The Decorative and Applied Art of Turkmenia*, Leningrad, 1976

Black, D., Loveless, C., *Rugs of the Wandering Baluchi*, London, 1976

Bogolyubov, A. A., *Carpets of Central Asia* (edited by J. M. A. Thompson), Fishguard, 1973

Bogolyubov, A. A., *Carpets of Central Asia*, St. Petersburg, 1908 [А. А. Боголюбов, *Ковры Средней Азии*, Санкт-Петербург, 1908]

Burdukov, N., *Guide to Carpets Displayed at the History Exhibition in the Museum of the Baron Stieglitz School*, St. Petersburg, 1904 [Н. Бурдуков, *Указатель по коврам, выставленным на исторической выставке в Музее Училища барона Штиглица*, Санкт-Петербург, 1904]

Cammann, Sch. V. R., "Symbolic Meanings in Oriental Rug Patterns: Parts I–III", *Textile Museum Journal*, vol. 3, 1972, pp. 5–66

Carpets of the Turkmen SSR, Moscow, 1952 [*Ковры Туркменской ССР*, Москва, 1952]

Clark, H., *Bokhara, Turkoman and Afghan Rugs*, London, 1922

Clark, H., "Turkoman Rugs: Two Prayer Rugs; Bokhara Proper and Saryk Turkoman", *The Connoisseur*, vol. 59, No. 235, March 1921, pp. 151–152

Cooper, Th., "An Ersari Germech", *Hali*, vol. 4, No. 2, 1981, pp. 151–152

Denny, W. B., *Oriental Rugs*, Washington, D.C., 1979

Dimand, M. S., Mailey, J., *Oriental Rugs in the Metropolitan Museum of Art*, New York, 1973

Dudin, S. M., "Carpet Products of Central Asia", *Anthology of the USSR Academy of Sciences Museum of Anthropology and Ethnography*, vol. 7, Leningrad, 1928, pp. 71–166 [С. М. Дудин, "Ковровые изделия Средней Азии", *Сборник Музея антропологии и этнографии АН СССР*, т. 7, Ленинград, 1928, с. 71–166]

Dzagurov, G., "Carpet Weaving in the Central Asian Republics", *The Manufacturing Cooperative*, No. 2, 1938 [Г. Дзагуров, "Ковроткачество в республиках Средней Азии", *Промысловая кооперация*, № 2, 1938]

Eiland, E., Shockley, M., *Tent Bands of the Steppes*, 1976

Eiland, M., *Oriental Rugs from Western Collection*, Berkley, 1973

Elliot-Pinner, L., "A Group of Ertmen Torba: Chodor or Yomut", *Hali*, vol. 2, No. 4, 1980, pp. 286–288

Erdmann, K., *The History of the Early Turkish Carpets*, London, 1977

The Ersari and Their Weavings, Christmas Exhibition of the International Hajji Baba Society, Washington, D.C., 1975

Farr, L., "A Turkoman Kap with the Panel Design", *Hali*, vol. 2, No. 4, 1980, p. 318

Felkerzam, A. A., "Old Carpets of Central Asia", *Old Years*, 1914, October–December; 1915, June [А. А. Фелькерзам, "Старинные ковры Средней Азии, *Старые годы*, 1914, октябрь–декабрь; 1915, июнь]

Gaube, H., "Die Teppiche der westturkmenischen Gruppe", *Mitteilungen der Societas Uralo-Altaica*, No. 1, 1968, pp. 45–62

Gavrilov, M. F., "The Art of Weaving of the Uzbek Women of the Village of Miliabad", *The National Economy of Central Asia*, Nos. 1–2, 1927 [М. Ф. Гаврилов, "Ткацкое искусство узбекской женщины с. Милябада", *Народное хозяйство Средней Азии*, 1927, № 1–2]

Gogel, F. A., *The Turkoman Carpet*, Moscow, 1927 [Ф. В. Гогель, *Туркменский ковер*, Москва, 1927]

Goguel, T. N., "Some Turkoman Carpets and Their Ornamentation", *Burlington Magazine for Connoisseurs*, vol. 50, No. 290, May 1927, pp. 251–254

Gombos, K., *Régi Türkmén Szőnyegek*, Budapest, 1975

Gombos, K., "The Turkoman Ensi in the Iparművészeti Museum", *Hali*, vol. 1, No. 4, 1979, pp. 345–348

Hoffmeister, P., and Crosby, A. S. B., *Turkoman Carpets in Franconia*, Edinburgh, 1980

Hollatz, G., "On Carpet Trails in the Nomad Areas of Central Asia", *Hali*, vol. 1, No. 2, 1978, pp. 142–148

Hopf, C., "Die Teppiche der Yomuden", *Antiquitätenzeitung*, Stuttgart, 1902

Irons, W., *The Yomut Turkmen*, Ann Arbor, 1969

Karamysheva, V. Kh., "Lokai Napramaches and Ilgiches", *Communications of the Republican Historical and Ethnographical Museum*, Issue 2, *History and Ethnography*, Stalinabad, 1955, pp. 121–160 [В. Х. Карамышева, "Локайские напрамачи и ильгичи", *Сообщения республиканского историко-краеведческого музея*, вып. 2, *История и этнография*, Сталинабад, 1955, с. 121–160]

Karpov, G. I., Arbekov, P. B., *Turkmenenforschung*, Band 1, Berlin, 1979

Klemm, Ye., "Art History Expedition to the Göklens", *Turkoman Studies*, Nos. 5–6, 1934 [Е. Клемм, "Искусствоведческая экспедиция к гокленам", *Туркменоведение*, № 5–6, 1934]

König, H., "Ersari Rugs—Names and Attribution", *Hali*, vol. 4, No. 2, 1981, pp. 135–141

König, H., "Some Ideas on the Design of Ersari Rugs and Their Origin", *Hali*, vol. 2, No. 4, 1980, pp. 275–282

Lefevre and Partners, *Central Asian Carpets*, London, 1976

Lefevre and Partners, *Central Asian Carpets, Supplement One, Rare Turkoman Weaving*, London, 1977

Leix, A., *Turkestan and Its Textile Crafts*, Hampshire, 1974

Loges, W., *Turkoman Tribal Rugs*, London, 1980

Macey, R. E. G., "Fine Rugs from Russian Turkestan", *Antiques Review II*, 1953, p. 25 ff

Mackie, L. W., Thompson, J., *Turkmen Tribal Carpets and Traditions*, Washington, D.C., 1980

Markov, G. E., "Sechs turkmenische Teppicherzeugnisse aus dem Museum für Völkerkunde zu Leipzig", *Jahrbuch des Museums für Völkerkunde zu Leipzig*, XIX, Leipzig, 1962, p. 120

McCoy, J. H., *Rugs of the Yomut Tribes*, Washington, D.C., 1970

McCoy, J. H., Boucher, J. W., *Weavings of the Tribes in Afghanistan, Washington Hajji Baba Society*, Washington, D.C., 1972

McCoy, J. H., Boucher, J. W., *Tribal Rugs from Turkmenistan, Washington Hajji Baba Society*, Washington, D.C., 1973

McCoy, J. H., Boucher, J. W., *Baluchi Rugs*, Washington, D.C., 1974

McCoy, J. H., Boucher, J. W., *Rugs of the Yomut Tribes, International Hajji Baba Society*, Washington, D.C., 1976

McCoy, J. H., Boucher, J. W., *Tribal Rugs from Turkmenistan, Christmas Exhibition of the International Hajji Baba Society*, Washington, D.C., 1973

McMullan, J. V., Reichert, D. O., *The George Walter Vincent and Belle Townsley Smith Collection of Islamic Rugs*, Springfield, 1970

Menzel, E., "Zeichnungen der Saryk-Teppiche", *Hali*, vol. 2, No. 4, 1980, pp. 282–286

Milhofer, S., *Die Teppiche Zentralasiens*, Hannover, 1968

Moshkova, V. G., "Tribal Göls in Turkoman Carpets", *Soviet Ethnography*, No. 1, 1946 [В. Г. Мошкова, "Племенные гёли в туркменских коврах, *Советская этнография*, № 1, 1946]

Moshkova, V. G., "Julkhyrses (Two Unique Nineteenth Century Uzbek Carpets from the Collection of the Uzbek Academy of Sciences History Museum)", *The Transactions of the History Museum of the Peoples of Uzbekistan*, issue 1: *Materials on History of the Peoples of Uzbekistan from the Museum Archives*, Tashkent, 1951, pp. 27–32 [В. Г. Мошкова, "Джульхырсы (два уникальных узбекских ковра XIX века из собрания Музея истории Академии наук УзбССР)", *Труды Музея истории народов Узбекистана*, вып. I: *Материалы к истории народов Узбекистана из фондов музея*, Ташкент, 1951, с. 27–32]

Moshkova, V. G., *Carpets and Rugs of the Peoples of Central Asia. Late 19th and Early 20th Centuries*, Tashkent, 1970 [В. Г. Мошкова, *Ковры народов Средней Азии. Конец XIX—начало XX века*, Ташкент, 1970]

Moshkova, V. G., "Tribal Göl in Turkoman Carpets", *Turkoman Studies I*, London, 1980, pp. 16–26

Moshkova, V. G., Morozova, A. S., "On History of Carpet Making in Merv", *Turkmen SSR Academy of Sciences Bulletin. Social Studies Series*, No. 1, 1961 [В. Г. Мошкова, А. С. Морозова, "К истории ковроделия Мерва", *Известия Академии наук ТуркмССР. Серия общественных наук*, № 1, 1961]

Mukanov, M. S., *The Kazakh Yurt*, Alma-Ata, 1981 [М. С. Муканов, *Казахская юрта*, Алма-Ата, 1981]

O'Bannon, G. W., "The Salitq Ersari Carpet", *Afghanistan Journal*, J. 4, No. 3, 1977, pp. 111–121

O'Bannon, G. W., *The Turkoman Carpet*, London, 1974

Pinner, R., "The Animal Tree and the Great Bird in Myth and Folklore", *Turkoman Studies I*, London, 1980, pp. 204–248

Pinner, R., Franses, M., "Some Interesting Tekke Products and Their Designs", *Turkoman Studies I*, London, 1980, pp. 102–163

Pinner, R., Franses, M., "Turkoman Khalyk", *Turkoman Studies I*, London, 1980, pp. 192–203

Pinner, R., Franses, M., "Two 'Turkoman' Carpets of the 15th Century", *Turkoman Studies I*, London, 1980, pp. 83–89

Pinner, R., Franses, M., King, D., "Turkoman Rugs in the Victoria and Albert Museum", *Hali*, vol. 2, No. 4, 1980, pp. 301–315

Pirkuliyeva, A. N., "Popular Decorative Art in Turkmenia of the Central Amu-Darya Towards the 19th and Early 20th Centuries", *Turkmen SSR Academy of Sciences Bulletin. Social Studies Series*, No. 4, 1964 [А. Н. Пиркулиева, "Народное декоративное искусство Туркмении Средней Аму-Дарьи к XIX—началу XX века", *Известия Академии наук ТуркмССР, Серия общественных наук*, № 4, 1964]

Ponomariov, O., "How the Turkoman Carpet is Made", *Turkoman Studies*, Nos. 10–12, 1931 [О. Пономарев, "Как делается туркменский ковер", *Туркменоведение*, № 10–12, 1931]

Ponomariov, O., "Three Moments", *Turkoman Studies*, Nos. 3–4, 1931 [О. Пономарев, "Три момента", *Туркменоведение*, № 3–4, 1931]

Ponomaryov, O., "The Motifs of Turkoman Carpets—The Salor, Tekke and Saryk", *Turkoman Studies I*, London, 1980, pp. 36–45

Prayer Rugs, The Textile Museum, Washington, D.C., 1974

Reed, S., *Oriental Rugs and Carpets*, London, 1967

Roberts, E. H., *Treasures from Near Eastern Looms*, Brunswick, 1981

Saurova, G., *The Turkmen Carpet of Today and Its Traditions*, Ashkhabad, 1968 [Г. Саурова, *Современный туркменский ковер и его традиции*, Ашхабад, 1968]

Schletzer, D., *Alte und antike Teppiche der Belutsch und Ersari*, Hamburg, 1974

Schürmann, U., *Central Asian Rugs*, London, 1969

Semionov, A. A., "The Carpets of Russian Turkestan. In Connection With the Edition of Carpet Pieces of Central Asia from Bogolyubov's Collection, St. Petersburg, 1907–8", *Ethnographical Review*, Nos. 1–2, 1911, pp. 137–179 [А. А. Семенов, "Ковры Русского Туркестана (По поводу издания "Ковровые изделия Средней Азии из собрания, составленного А. А. Боголюбовым", Санкт-Петербург, 1907–1908)", *Этнографическое обозрение*, № 1–2, 1911, с. 137–179]

Sienknecht, H., "Turkmenische Knüpfarbeiten im Lübecker Museum für Völkerkunde", *Hali*, vol. 1, No 1, 1978, pp. 23–35

Simakov, N., "The Art of Central Asia", *Turkoman Studies I*, London, 1980, pp. 7–11

Thacher, A. B., *Turkoman Rugs*, New York, 1940, reprinted London, 1977

Tikhonovich, V., "The Culture of Ornamentation of the Turkoman Carpet", *Turkoman Studies*, Nos. 4–5, 1930 [В. Тихонович, "Культура орнамента туркменского ковра", *Туркменоведение*, № 4–5, 1930]

Transactions of the Kirghiz Archeological and Ethnographical Expedition, vol. 5, Moscow, 1968 [*Труды киргизской археолого-этнографической экспедиции*, т. 5, Москва, 1968]

Tzareva, E., "Saryk Tent Bags in the State Museum of Ethnography of the Peoples of the USSR", *Hali*, vol. 1, No. 3, 1978, pp. 277–280

Wagner, W., "Das Kleeblatt-Motiv auf turkmenischen Teppichen", *Heimtex*, 1968/8, pp. 130–132

Wagner, W., "Die Rhomben-Spirale etc.", *Heimtex*, 1969/5, p. 159 ff

Wagner, W., "Ein seltener Tekke", *Heimtex*, 1969/8, p. 153 ff

Wagner, W., Schürmann, U., "Zentralasiatische Teppiche", *Heimtex*, 1970/1, pp. 119–120; 1970/2, p. 262

Whiting, M., "The Dyes of Turkoman Rugs", *Hali*, vol. 1, No. 3, 1978, pp. 281–283

Whiting, M., "Tent Bags and Simple Statistics", *Turkoman Studies I*, London, 1980, pp. 90–95

Yelkovich, L., "On the Themes of Turkmen Carpets", *Decorative Art*, No. 6, 1958 [Л. Елькович, "О сюжетно-тематических туркменских коврах", *Декоративное искусство*, № 6, 1958]

Zhdanko, T. A., "Popular Ornamental Art of the Karakalpak. Studies of Karakalpak Ethnography", in: *Transactions of the Khoresm Archaeological and Ethnographical Expedition*, vol. 3, Moscow, 1958, pp. 373–410 [Т. А. Жданко, "Народное орнаментальное искусство каракалпаков. Материалы и исследования по этнографии каракалпаков", в кн.: *Труды хорезмской археолого-этнографической экспедиции*, т. 3, Москва, 1958, с. 373–410]

КОВРЫ СРЕДНЕЙ АЗИИ И КАЗАХСТАНА
Альбом (на английском языке)

Издательство „Аврора". Ленинград. 1984
Изд. № 85

Printed and bound in Austria by Globus, Vienna